# Friends
## AND
# Frenemies

# Friends
## AND
# Frenemies

## THE GOOD, THE BAD, AND THE AWKWARD

BY
JENNIFER CASTLE
AND
DEBORAH REBER

ILLUSTRATIONS BY
KAELA GRAHAM

## ZEST BOOKS
San Francisco

# ZEST BOOKS

**Connect with Zest!**

- zestbooks.net/blog
- zestbooks.net/contests
- twitter.com/zestbooks

- facebook.com/zestbook
- facebook.com/BooksWithATwist
- pinterest.com/zestbooks

35 Stillman Street, Suite 121, San Francisco, CA 94107 / www.zestbooks.net

Manufactured in China
SCP 10 9 8 7 6 5 4 3 2 1
4500531828

# TABLE OF CONTENTS

# INTRODUCTION

## Friends are the family we choose.

Do you agree?

If so, maybe it's because:

## Friends can love and support us just like family members do.

And also because:

## Friendships, just like relationships with parents and siblings, are never simple.

Yes, friendship is fabulous, fantastic, and so much fun. But yes, it can also be mysterious, unpredictable, and even painful.

**Have you ever found yourself wondering...**

- How can I make friends?
- How can I find that one great BFF and be a good friend to him or her?
- How can I help a friend in need?
- Why do friends fight and how can I handle it?
- Why do friends gossip and spread rumors?
- Can boys and girls be friends with each other?
- When one moves away, how can two friends stay in touch?
- How do you know when to end a friendship, and what's the best way to do it?

You have? Good! Because these are really important questions. Fortunately, we've got answers! This book tackles all these topics and more, with information and advice from experts, other tweens, and teen "mentors" to help you explore the how's, why's, and how-to's of these special people in our lives.

## Who Are These "Mentors," Anyway?

The Mentors sharing their comments and advice throughout this book are teenagers who've recently been through some of the same things you're experiencing right now. They're a little older, and a little wiser, and can share what they've learned with you.

Ready to read on, dig in, and listen up?

# Okay... LET'S GO!

# CHAPTER 1

# WHAT IS A FRIEND?

**M**aybe you and your BFF are attached at the hip. Or maybe you don't really have one "best friend," but lots of different people you have fun with. It could be that you don't have any close friends at the moment but are definitely on the lookout for some. If any of those friendship situations sounds like yours, you're not alone. A "best friend" can be hard to come by, and the definition of a best friend varies depending on whom you ask. Getting a best friend has very little to do with you as a person and A LOT to do with getting to know the right person at the right time. You're bound to meet someone you really click with eventually. In the meantime, it helps to know what you're looking for in any kind of friendship — best friend or not. Remember that a friend doesn't have to be "best" to add something really special to your life.

# "What do you like most about your friend?"

"*She's always there for me.* If I'm in a bad situation, she always has ideas and suggestions up her sleeve. She's like an older sister who I can look up to."

**—MEGAN, 10**

"*She's loyal and trustworthy.* I can tell her anything, and don't have to worry about her telling anyone. She knows when to use her sense of humor and when to be sympathetic. Also, she can turn something that's sad or upsetting into something funny and joyful."

**—KATE, 12**

"The thing I like most about my friend is that **he makes me laugh.** We make each other laugh so hard that we can't breathe!"

**—ANDREW, 13**

"*My friend is always there when I need her.* Her positive attitude makes me feel happy, she always has something nice to say, and she always makes me laugh.

**—CAROLINE, 12**

*"We have a lot of things in common, like eating the same foods, liking the same actors or actresses, shopping, watching movies, and just talking! I love being around her because I can tell her my problems, and then I don't feel so stressed out about middle school and other things."*

**—ALYSSA, 11**

*"What I like about my friend is that she is the opposite of me! She and I are totally different and I like to hear our different opinions."*

**—KORTNI, 11**

*"What I like about my friend is that she's friendly, trusting, nice, and also has my back. I'm always there for her and she will always be there for me."*

**—STEPHANIE, 9**

Starting to see a pattern here? Friends are people who make you feel good about yourself. They're people who like you for who you are, support you through good times and bad... and tell you if you have a big chunk of spinach in your teeth.

## From the Mentors

A friend is a person who likes you for who you are inside, not what you look like on the outside. A friend is someone you want to be with, and not for any particular reason — just to be with them. One of my favorite quotes about best friends is:

*"What is a friend? A single soul dwelling in two bodies."*

—ARISTOTLE

I think this sums up what my best friend and I are. **— LEAH**

# What Makes a Good Friend?

Because we're all different, we all want different things from our friendships, but there are several qualities that rank pretty high on everyone's list of friend "must-haves":

**Trustworthiness**: This one is a biggie. When you have a friend you can really trust with your innermost secrets, no matter how personal or embarrassing, that's a friend to hold on to.

**Honesty**: Friends who tell you the truth, whatever the situation is or however difficult it might be, are the kind you want to surround yourself with. If a friend is honest with you no matter what, your relationship has an excellent chance of surviving through thick and thin.

**Loyalty**: When friends are loyal, they've always got your back. Friends who will stand up for you in a difficult situation are worth their weight in gold.

**Reliability**: Everyone wants a friend to count on to be there during life's ups and downs. When you're going through a hard time, or even when you have something you want to celebrate, a good friend will be by your side.

**A Sense of Humor**: Sometimes it's nice to just let loose, blast your favorite song, and have a big ol' spazz attack. When you do, who better to share it with than a friend whose sense of humor is just as wacky as your own?

**Openness**: If you can't speak your mind without worrying that your friend will judge or criticize you, what's the point of saying what you think? True friends allow each other to be completely open. Even if she doesn't always agree with your point of view, your friend should respect you enough to hear you out.

**Common Interests**: These are often what bring about the start of a friendship... and they're just as important for keeping it strong. Having a friend who shares your passion for soccer or eating stale marshmallow Peeps can be the tie that binds.

**Common Sense**: Sometimes you need an outside point of view on a situation, and if you're not up for going to a parent or sibling, a friend is another place to turn. When you do, you'll want some good practical advice, which hopefully your pal can give to you... or at least she can show you another way to look at the problem.

**Genuineness**: Most importantly, friends should like you for who you are, not which social group you're in, how much money you have, or how you dress. Friends who you can be yourself around are true keepers.

## Remember...

Friendships go both ways. If these qualities are important for your friends to have, it's just as important for you to have them, too.

# Things that DON'T Define a Friend

Do you have friendships where every so often (or maybe quite often) something doesn't feel right? It can be easy to define friends as the people you hang out with, good or bad, but check out the list of qualities below. If they describe what's happening with one of your friends, you might want to give your friendship a closer look. Reconsider being friends with someone if he or she:

**Pressures you**: Sure, it's natural for friends to want you to be interested in the same things they are. But it's NOT cool for a friend to tell you what to do or make you feel bad for not doing exactly what she wants. Friends who pressure you into something you don't want aren't worth having around.

**Disrespects or ridicules you**: Are you the butt of every joke at the cafeteria table? Does your friend make fun of you just to get a laugh out of everyone else and make himself look cooler? These are signs of an unhealthy friendship.

**Gossips**: Friends don't gossip behind friends' backs. A true friend will be the one to stop the gossip, or stick up for you if there's a rumor about you going around.

**Manipulates you or others**: Do you have a friend who has "power" over you? Does she make you feel guilty for being who you are? Does she use others in your group of friends to make you do something? Does she know just how to push your buttons, and do it often? If the answer to any of these questions is "yes," your friend is manipulating you and possibly others. This is sneaky, unkind, and not a characteristic of a good friend.

**Clings too close:** Friends know when to give each other room... room to breathe, room to grow, and room to explore. If your friend is threatened when you take time for yourself, she might be insecure about her role in the friendship, which can make things awkward for you. Wanting to be with you every second of every day isn't necessarily the sign of a healthy connection.

**Is jealous or competitive:** Because friends are often interested in the same things — sports, hobbies, crushes —little jealousies or competitions can creep up and get between you and your BFF. Nip these in the bud. If you're competing with your friend, you aren't going to be able to support him like a good friend should, and vice versa.

## From the Mentors

I think it is really important to just BE there for a friend. Sometimes even words are unnecessary; just your presence will cheer up your friend's day. And if I have toilet paper stuck to my shoe, I would want my friends to tell me. What I really like about my close circle of friends is that they never put any peer pressure on me, like me for who I am, and respect my choices. **— JOYCE**

To me a friend is a person who you trust and can rely on. He or she is someone you can actually spend time with and who feels the same way you feel about them. If you ever need them, they're there for you to talk to, spend time with, or just hang out with. The best qualities in a friend are always being able to talk to him or her about anything, and always being able to turn to that person in times of need. Those are the friends to hold on to. **— JARON**

# Different Kinds of Friendships

Think about all of your friends. Does each friendship look exactly the same? Probably not... and that's healthy! The types of friends you have can vary, depending on what's going on in your life, what your hobbies or interests are at the time, and so on. Here are just a few of the different types of friendships.

**BFFs and CLOSE FRIENDS are the ones who...** you can spend hours and hours with, holed up in your room, gabbing on the phone, or texting at light speed. You trust them with your most closely held secrets. They watch your back when the bad times come, share your obsession with cheese fries, aren't horrified if soda comes out of your nose when you're laughing, and understand how you're feeling even if you haven't said a word.

**SOCIAL FRIENDS are the ones who...** are in your wider circle of friends. You share some common interests, but they might not be the first ones you turn to when you're having a hard day. They're fun to hang out with every now and then.

**CASUAL ACQUAINTANCES are the ones who...** you may not hang out with outside of school, but you say "hello" in the hallway and talk about the horror of the math quiz after class.

**MENTORS are the ones who...** you look up to, usually because they're a lot older and have some qualities (athletic, academic, or social) that you admire and want to learn from.

**PROTÉGÉS are the ones who...** might be younger than you, so they look up to and admire you for who you are!

This list just scratches the surface of the kinds of friends you might have. No two friends will bring the same things into your life. That's one of the great things about building friendships with different people! The wider variety of relationships you have, the more fulfilled you'll likely find yourself.

## From the Mentors

A friend is a person who comforts you when you're in need, who you can trust in any situation, and who supports you with every decision you make. Friends are people who can make you smile when you're down. All of my closest friends are generous and caring, which makes them easy and fun to be around. — **DANIELLE**

# The Journal Is Your Friend

One of the best ways you can sort out your emotions and experiences related to friendship — and anything, really — is to keep a journal. Even if you've never written in a journal before or don't think of yourself as a "writer," you should still give it a try. Some tips to get you started:

Get yourself a journal. It can be one that comes with a cool cover, or it can be a plain notebook you decorate with drawings, stickers, or anything else that makes it your own. It can be big, little, lined, or unlined. If it's got pages, it fits the bill.

**Experiment with different writing utensils.** Pen, pencil, marker, whatever. Anything goes!

**Find a quiet, private place.** Maybe that's in your room, at the school library, or that comfy spot between the couch and window. If one location isn't working for you, try another.

Throughout this book, we'll be offering up questions and sentence beginnings that will "kickstart" your journaling. **Copy down each kickstart and then let your thoughts take you from there.**

## JOURNAL KICKSTART! What is a Friend?

- The qualities I look for in a friend are...
- My three favorite qualities in my friends are...
- The three great qualities I offer my friends are...
- One situation where I really came through for a friend was...

# Try this one with a friend!

**Instructions:** Take a blank page from your journal or a separate sheet of paper. Fold it in half down the middle and copy down this checklist on both sides. Fill out your answers, then turn it over and have your friend fill out new answers on the other side. When you're both done, unfold the paper and compare what each of you checked off!

**The four friendship qualities that are most important to me are:**

- Trust
- Honesty
- Loyalty
- Reliability
- Sense of humor
- Openness
- Practicality
- Authenticity
- Common interests

**The four qualities that I'm most able to give my friends are:**

- Trust
- Honesty
- Loyalty
- Reliability
- Sense of humor
- Openness
- Practicality
- Authenticity
- Common interests

**The four friendship qualities that are most important to me are:**

- Trust
- Honesty
- Loyalty
- Reliability
- Sense of humor
- Openness
- Practicality
- Authenticity
- Common interests

**The four qualities that I'm most able to give my friends are:**

- Trust
- Honesty
- Loyalty
- Reliability
- Sense of humor
- Openness
- Practicality
- Authenticity
- Common interests

## Remember...

- Good friends are ones who are trustworthy, honest, loyal, reliable, open, and most importantly, *like you for who you are.*

- Not-so-good friends are ones who pressure you, disrespect you, gossip about you, or who are manipulative, clingy, and competitive.

- Friendships go both ways... the qualities you look for in a friend are the qualities that you should be offering, too.

- No two friendships are alike... there's room for all different kinds of relationships, and they all bring something unique to your life!

## Bottom line:

# Friends are people who make you feel good about yourself.

# CHAPTER 2

# MAKING FRIENDS

**M**aybe you're starting at a new school, or it's the first day of summer camp and you don't know a soul. Maybe you've outgrown your old friends (or they've outgrown you), and you're feeling like your social circle could be wider. Now what?

# Tips for Launching New Friendships

Making new friends can take some effort — and a little self-confidence, too — but it's absolutely worth it. Here's a good place to start!

**Always be yourself**: People can be tempted to do and say some crazy things in order to fit in with a new friend or social group. Unfortunately, this doesn't result in true friendship. Will you ever really be comfortable around these people if you're pretending to be someone you're not? And how long can you keep up the charade, anyway? In a real friendship, there's no acting, no pretending, no hiding. Be yourself from the start and you'll form deeper, more honest friendships.

**Talk to people and be friendly:** This can be especially hard if you're shy. But being friendly doesn't mean you have to walk around school wearing a T-shirt that says, *"Hey, don't you want to talk to ME?"* It can be as simple as smiling at people when you pass them in the hallway, or saying "hello" to the person next to you in class, or complimenting someone on her new haircut. If you're open and seem easy to approach, you'll become the kind of person that others want to be around.

**Learn how to listen**: Have you ever noticed that most people *love* to talk about themselves? It might be their favorite sports, their hobbies, their dog... *whatever*. If you're a good listener, you'll be surprised at how many people are drawn to you. By asking questions and listening carefully to the answers, your new friends will feel the genuine interest you have in them. And they'll want to give it right back to you.

**Let others know you like them:** How many times have you been involved in an argument because a friend completely misunderstood what you said or meant? The same kind of thing can happen with potential friendships. Sometimes people assume you don't like them, so even if they really do want to be your friend, they figure you're not interested. If you've found someone you want to be friends with, let him or her know. No megaphones or billboards necessary. It's the little things that count: saving a seat for your friend on the bus, bringing in an extra cupcake for lunch, or remembering to wish him or her good luck before a big test.

**Put your new friendships on "project status":** If making new friends is something you really want to do, then you have to make it a priority. Just like improving in a sport or getting better grades, making new friends takes time and energy, so set aside some each day or week to devote to your new friendships.

**Be patient:** Friendships that are formed in a day sometimes only last that long. Developing solid friendships can take time, but that's okay. The more time you both spend getting to know each other and building a solid foundation, the less likely it is that your friendship will crumble at the first sign of trouble.

## From the Mentors

The easiest way to make a friend is to just take a chance. If you meet someone you could see being friends with, talk to him and try to get to know him. And always remember to be yourself, because a friend should like you for who you are and not for something you aren't. **— JARON**

# Help Wanted: One BFF — Loyal, Trusting, Fun to Be With

In search of a BFF? Sometimes it seems like everyone in the world has one. You know, the kind who would do anything to get you out of a jam.

But what if you don't have a BFF? Is there something wrong with you? Absolutely not. You never know when these close friends, the ones who'll stick with you through thick and thin, will come into your life. But there's no point in forcing the issue or trying to create a BFF out of someone just because she's there. When these friendships do form naturally, they're usually the real thing... and they're always worth the wait.

On the other hand, you might already have a friend who's close enough to be considered a BFF, but you've never thought of her that way before. Think about the friends you have, what your relationships with them are like, and how they treat you. Maybe you'll develop a deeper appreciation for someone you've always thought of as just another acquaintance. She might be a better friend than you think!

## From the Mentors
To make new friends, don't try to be popular or someone you're not, because it doesn't work. Let the kids around you see you for who you are. — **LAURA**

# What NOT to Do:

**DON'T be a gossip:** Spreading gossip and rumors about someone else might seem like a great way to get the attention of new friends, but don't be fooled. Even if people are interested in the dirt you have to dish, they'll probably see you as someone who's not trustworthy. If you're so willing to talk about other people behind their backs, what's to stop them from doing the same to you? Stay out of the nasty cycle of gossip.

**DON'T play games:** We're not talking about *Twister* and *Cranium* here. We're talking about the games we sometimes play with people's minds to get them to feel or do what we want. If this is usually your strategy, think twice before rolling the dice. The way you act in the beginning of a relationship will lay the foundation for the friendship to come. Stick to honesty and straightforwardness, and you and your new pal will be off on the right foot.

**DON'T force yourself on anyone**: You know those people who insist on hanging around you, maybe even hanging *onto* you, when you really just need some space? Sometimes when people are desperate to make a friendship work, they'll force themselves into situations where they're not really welcome. Leave the clinginess to Velcro. Your friends should be just as happy to spend time with you as you are to hang out with them.

**DON'T forget personal hygiene:** During your middle-school years, people's bodies start going through unexpected changes. Maybe you're sweating more than you used to, or your hair is getting greasy more quickly. That's normal... but you may want to talk to a parent about bathing habits and products like deodorant. In a perfect world, it shouldn't matter what you look or smell like; but in the real world, these things can keep you from making the new friendships you seek.

# Operation: Outgoing

Is there someone out there you'd like to get to know better, maybe at school or in an extracurricular activity? Think about people you'd like to be more outgoing with, and which of these "friendliness tactics" seem most natural to you:

- Generally being friendly, as in: "I like your hair that length!"; "Nice shirt!"; and "Hi!"
- Acting interested in a person's life, such as: "Is that a picture of your dog? What's its name?"; "I heard you're taking dance lessons. What kind? Do you like it?"; and "Did you see anything good on TV over the weekend?"
- Pointing out the things you have in common, like: "Hey, I read that book, too. Good stuff, eh?" or "Nice Yankees cap. Are you a fan? So am I!"
- Doing something nice, as in: offering a spare piece of gum or saving a space in line.

## Focus on Shyness

Are you a shy person? If you are, being faced with the challenge of making a new friend can seem scarier than climbing Mount Everest. But believe it or not, one of the best ways to overcome shyness in social situations is to put yourself right in the middle of them. Set small goals for yourself, like saying "hi" or smiling to a different person each day. Paralyzed at the thought of picking up the phone to call someone? Script out what you're going to say first and read it through. Lastly, try pretending for a day that you're not shy. What would that be like? You might find that people respond to you in very positive ways, and at the same time, you'll build the self-confidence you need to put yourself out there more often.

# Where to Meet New Friends

Where can you find these future besties? Besides the usual places (classes, the cafeteria, the school bus), here are some other options for finding new friends:

**After-school activities:** The great thing about meeting new friends here is that, chances are, you'll have at least one thing in common right off the bat with the people you come across. If you love to act, drama club is the perfect place to find other drama queens (and kings) who share your love of the stage. Or if building stuff is your thing, you can build *connections* with fellow members of a Robotics or Lego club. Think about how easy it is to be yourself in these environments, and go for it!

**Sports teams:** Being involved in athletics is a great way to meet friends, especially if the sport you're participating in is a team sport. You'll be pushed to work together, communicate, cheer, and support each other on a deeper level.

**Volunteering:** Do you walk shelter dogs in your spare time? Help clean up parks? Paint murals on the walls of local schools? There are tons of volunteer opportunities available to you, and they're great ways to make new friends. You know that the people you meet while volunteering will not only share your passion for whatever the activity is, but also for helping others.

**Religious youth groups:** If your place of worship has a youth group, you might find that great friendships start there. Youth groups often host cool activities like bowling nights, movie outings, and other get-togethers, so there'll be plenty of opportunities for socializing.

# It's Your Turn!

So now that you've read through our advice, here's your chance to come up with your own words of wisdom! Pretend you're the advice columnist for your school newspaper. Copy down this question in your journal and write a response:

*This year I started going to a new school. People here are different than those at my old school. They all have a lot of money and don't want to make new friends. What can I do to fit in here?* **—MARTIN, 11**

## From the Mentors

I usually meet friends in school, in my neighborhood, or through other friends. After a new friend and I have seen and talked regularly and become comfortable with each other, we'll start hanging out together in our spare time. I think the best advice for making friends is to not force yourself on anybody. If someone likes you and wants to be your friend, then you'll eventually become friends. But if you try too hard for someone to like you, you'll drive that person away. **— LEAH**

Making friends is not something that happens overnight. It takes time. I think the best way to make friends is to talk to people and get to know them. Sometimes friendships happen when you're not looking for them. They'll turn up in the most unlikely places! **—MEGAN**

# Quotes From Kids Like You

*"I try to mingle with kids. If that doesn't work, I try to show my athletic skills (or something I'm really good at)."*

**—DUCHANA, 11**

*"I talk and listen and ask them questions about themselves. Most importantly, I try to be nice."*

**—K.J., 9**

***"First of all, you have to be a little outgoing.*** *Find a kid who's standing by herself and go over and talk to her. She's probably new. Nobody needs friends more than the new kid at school."*

**—ALLEY, 11**

***"A friend is someone you feel comfortable with, not someone you have to put on a show for!"***

**—OLIVIA, 12**

***"Just be open!*** *Also, don't always wait for people to come to you!"*

**—SHAKOA, 12**

## Remember...

Friendships can develop where you least expect them, so be open! You never know when your next great friend will come along!

*"My first week as the new kid, I was really lonely.* After a while, I noticed a kid getting bullied around. I went and helped him overcome the bullies and now I'm his friend."

**—JAMES, 13**

*"Just get involved!* If there's a certain hobby or sport that interests you, dive right in! It's a great way to meet friends and have a lot of fun!"

**—KATE, 13**

# Making Friends

Want to think deeper and express yourself about this chapter? Open up your journal, write down one or more of these sentence starters, and then see where your words and feelings take you.

- My friend _____ and I became friends when...
- If I wanted to make new friends now I would...
- One thing I might do differently in order to make new friends is...
- Some of the qualities that make me a good friend to others are...
- The most unusual place I made a new friend was...

## The Votes Are In

Where is the best place to make new friends?

**School: 73%   Sports: 14%**
After-school activities: 13%

## From the Mentors

I have made new friends by talking to people in class about something we both like. I've also made friends through different afterschool activities. This is an especially cool place to meet friends because you already have at least one thing in common! If you're not sure how to make new friends, get involved in something you enjoy, and just start talking to people involved in it too. **—TIFFANY**

## Remember...

- When looking to make new friends, always be yourself!

- If making a new friend is a priority for you, put it on "project status." Set goals just like you would for acing a test or perfecting your softball swing.

- BFFs don't come along every day, so don't try to force the issue with a potential friend. Friendships that develop over time usually have the most solid foundation.

- If you're shy, set small goals, like saying "hi" to one new person every day, or calling a potential friend once every week.

- If meeting new friends is your goal, go out there and get involved! Friendships spring out of shared interests, hobbies, sports, and other activities.

- Friendships can develop where you least expect them... so be open!

(Don't forget to wear deodorant and bathe often.)

## CHAPTER 3

# WHEN FRIENDS FIGHT

Fun. Trust. Love. These are all normal parts of friendship. You know what's also normal? Arguing and fighting. They just come with being human.

# Arguing...

...is when you and your friends are expressing opposing ideas or opinions, or trying to come to an agreement about something specific. Arguing happens because you're honest with, and care about, one another. You're communicating. That's all good.

# Fighting...

...on the other hand... well, fighting means people are angry, or hurt, or communication has totally broken down. Usually it means all of the above, and that is definitely *not* good. Fights can start over little things ("I can't believe you bought the same pair of jeans I just wore!!") or big stuff ("How could you invite everyone to your sleepover but me?").

Here are the most common causes of conflict in a friendship. How many have you experienced?

• Jealousy (anything from envying your friend's lacrosse skills to wishing your outfit looked as effortlessly cool as theirs)
• Being excluded
• A friend breaking a trust
• Gossiping and rumors (see Chapter 4)
• Talking behind each other's backs
• Crushing on the same person

A fight doesn't have to be the end of the world, or even the end of the friendship. In fact, bumpy patches can make a friendship stronger. It all depends on how you deal with them! A good rule of thumb for surviving a BFF blow-up is: **Think. Talk. Apologize. Move On**. Are you ready to make up, not break up?

# THINK. Talk.
# Apologize.
# Move On.

Picture this. You told your best friend a secret and she swore not to tell another soul. But by the end of the day, half the school is in on the dirt. Sound familiar? If your answer is *yes*, chances are that the way you felt about this — confused, angry, frustrated, sad — is familiar, too. When these kinds of emotions are involved, stop and take the time to **think** before you do anything.

*Think about what*, you ask? Good question. Just *thinking* about how annoyed you are is only going to get you more worked up. Instead, ask yourself these questions:

**How did the fight start?** What exactly happened? When did it really start? How did things get out of control? Try to get a sense of the big picture.

**What was MY part in this fight?** This can be a tricky one. It doesn't matter who "started it." But take a close, honest look at how your actions — and reactions — may have gotten you to this point.

**Have either of us done things to make it worse?** This can tell you a great deal about how healthy your friendship really is. If you and your friend fight a lot, chances are that you both handled this fight like you have in the past.

**What exactly am I feeling?** Sorting out complicated feelings takes time and practice. When you're fighting with a friend, emotions like anger, jealousy, frustration, and sadness tend to get all mixed up in a jumbled mess. Break this question down into little ones, such as:

• How did I feel when the fight began?
• How do I feel at this moment?
• Have I felt this way before with the same friend? When?

**What is the friend I'm fighting with feeling?** Okay, so you probably can't read minds, but actions say a lot about what's going on inside someone's head. Look at your friend. Does he give you angry looks even though he's trying to act cool? Does she seem about to burst into tears every time she sees you? Does he make comments that sound like nice statements but really end up being digs at you? What do those things tell you about your friend's feelings?

**Am I just hanging on to my anger?** It can be hard to let go of angry feelings, but ask yourself, "Is this anger actually helping me, or hurting me?"

**Do you still remember what you're fighting about?** Some fights drag on for so long that you have to ask yourself, "Are we really still fighting over something real, or are we just fighting for the sake of argument now?

**Writing helps us organize our thoughts!** Grab your journal and record your answers to these questions whenever you're arguing with a friend.

## Here's what could go wrong if you DON'T take the time to think:

- You might say something that you don't mean out of anger.
- You might further damage the relationship.
- You might embarrass yourself.
- You might feel bad later about how you handled the situation.

## On the other hand, here's what could happen when you DO take time to think:

- You can figure out what's really going on.
- You can address the situation with your emotions in control.
- You can settle the fight in a mature way.
- You can feel good knowing that you kept your cool.

## Remember...

Don't take responsibility for your friend's feelings! We all deal with tough situations differently. The best thing you can do is to sort out what's happening in your own head and be ready to listen to your friend's point of view.

# Think. TALK. Apologize. Move On.

So now that you've thought things out, it's time to take the next step. That's right: like it or not, you've got to do some *talking*. It can be nerve-wracking and scary, though, so here are some tips for getting started:

## How to Get the Words Out

- **In person:** Always the best bet (but usually the scariest, too), talking with your friend one-on-one is the most direct way of saying what you need to say.
- **On the phone:** This isn't a bad second option if you're worried about being too flustered for the face-to-face talk. Also, you can write down your main points and refer to them throughout the conversation if you need to.
- **In a letter:** Sometimes fights get so messy and confusing that it's easier to get your thoughts out on paper. This way you can freely express yourself and make sure that you say everything you want to. See the section on *I-Messages* for tips.
- **Over e-mail or text message:** If you and your friend are both online, you might be tempted to settle things on the Internet. Be careful! Feelings can get lost in a digital setting, no matter how many emoticons you use. Your words might be misunderstood or you might find yourself hitting the "send" button before you meant to.

# What to Say

However you've decided to approach your friend, you've got to choose your words... and choose them carefully. To get to the heart of the matter, try a technique called "I-Messages." This will help you figure out a way to get your point across clearly, hopefully without upsetting your friend. All you need to do is answer these three questions as honestly as possible:

1. **I feel...** _____
2. **when you...** _____
3. because... _____.

Make sense? Here's an example of how it might work:

1. **I feel...** lonely and angry
   *(Be as specific as you can about your emotions, and use as many words as you need to describe how you feel.)*
2. **when you...** spend more time with other friends
   *(Give details here about how your friend has acted or what he or she has done.)*
3. because... I don't know why we can't all hang out together.
   *(This is the hard one: the "why" of the problem. Give it some thought!)*

**Put it all together:** "I feel lonely and angry when you spend more time with other friends, because I don't know why we can't all hang out together."

### Why Do I-Messages Work?
- You take responsibility for your feelings.
- You don't blame the other person.
- You get your point across clearly and briefly.
- They can sometimes offer solutions to the problem.

# In·Person Pointers

Going face-to-face? Good for you! Here are some things to keep in mind:

- **Choose the right time and place.** Approaching your friend between classes in the school hallway, restroom, or crowded cafeteria? Uh, probably not a good idea. You'll have more luck in a private, comfortable, non-rushed situation. If you can, arrange a meetup ahead of time so your friend doesn't feel ambushed.
- **Stay cool and calm:** Before you start talking, take a few deep breaths and promise yourself to keep the volume low. If you sense you're raising your voice, it's time to take another deep breath. Don't be in a hurry to say what you have to say, and don't rush your friend either.
- **Listen, listen, listen:** Conversations are two-way streets. Ask your friend to let you speak without interruption, and give him or her the same courtesy.
- **Avoid the blame game:** ...even if a fight seems to be more one person's fault than the other's. This doesn't only apply to the other person. Don't take the blame for the entire situation yourself, either. Instead, focus on the emotions you're both feeling, and why you're feeling that way. If you find yourself slipping into accusations, catch yourself and stop.

## The Votes Are In
What do you do when a friend hurts your feelings?

**Talk it over: 62%    Forget about it: 21%**
Stop being his or her friend: 17%

## Still Having Trouble?

If it feels like you and your friend have hit a wall or are going around in circles, it's time to call for backup. Talk to a teacher, school counselor, or other neutral authority figure about helping you and your friend work out your differences. School counselors and social workers are experts at this stuff, and going to them for help is a way of (a) having someone help you look at the problem from a neutral point of view, and (b) learning more about how to deal with fights in the future.

Your parents or older siblings can be leaned on, too. If you ask them, you'll probably find that they've been in a similar situation at some point. If you're a little unsure about how to bring things up, try asking them some of these questions:

- Did you ever get into fights with friends when you were younger?
- Did you stay friends or end the friendship?
- If you made up, how did you get over the fight?
- Do you still fight with your friends?
- How do you resolve the fights you have today?
- How can I talk with my friend without making things worse?

### From the Mentors

My friend and I solve our disputes by remembering that we're not perfect, and that we're supposed to be different from each other. —**JESSICA**

### Remember...

Once you write something down and hand it over, those words are there for good. Write your letter, email, or text carefully — and do a rough draft or two if you need to!

# Think. Talk. APOLOGIZE. Move On.

**"I'm sorry."** These can be the two hardest words on the planet to utter, but unless you and your friend both say them, your friendship won't have as much of a chance of getting to where you want it to be. Apologizing doesn't have to be torture for you or your friend. But it has to be sincere, because saying the phrase sarcastically or angrily doesn't hold much weight. If you mean what you're saying, you should get the result you want. Here are some things to keep in mind:

## It's Not About Winning

We all love to be right, and when two friends are fighting, it's easy to think the other is to blame. But saying "I'm sorry" doesn't mean that you "lose." It means stepping up to the plate and taking responsibility for your role in what went wrong. If your focus is on "winning" the fight, then it is more likely that both of you will end up "losing."

## Remember...

When it's your friend's turn to speak, concentrate on keeping your lips together. You can react with nods and shakes of your head, but try and refrain from saying anything that might come across as an interruption. When you think your friend is done talking, count to 10 in your head before responding to make sure she doesn't have anything to add.

## Take the First Step

This shows that the friendship is important enough to you that you want to save it. But what if your friend is mostly responsible for the problem? Should you apologize for something you didn't do? No! But when you reflect on the situation, find something that you *did* do to take responsibility for. Maybe you overreacted to what your friend did, or got other friends involved in the fight. Whatever it is, there is a part of the fight that you own. Relationships are about two people. Each person plays a part in what happens, good *and* bad.

## Tips for Apologizing

A little preparation can go a long way. If you're unsure about how to apologize, try using one of the sentences below:

- "I feel really bad about _____, and I'm sorry that it happened."
- "I know you've felt _____, and I'm sorry for making you feel that way."

Notice how there's no finger-pointing going on anywhere in those sentences? Try to keep apologies simple! This makes it less likely that the discussion will go to a negative place.

## Remember...

If your friend doesn't apologize, or thinks that he or she has "won" just because you apologized first, then this person is not ready to make up yet.

IMPORTANT! There are special circumstances where you shouldn't be the one to apologize first, like if your friend physically hurt you or did something that put you in danger. Apologizing first might give your friend the impression that he has power or control over you. This is actually bullying, not friendship.

# Think. Talk. Apologize.
# MOVE ON.

So? How did it go? If you've followed the above guidelines of *think, talk,* and *apologize,* and your friend was a willing participant, hopefully you're both ready for the next and final step in our plan: *making up and moving on.* Are things still a little awkward between the two of you? That's normal, especially if your fight has lasted a couple of days or weeks, or even longer. Give it time, and follow these tips:

## Rediscover What Made You Friends

Is it a love of singing that you both share? Maybe you're both obsessed with your dogs. Whatever it is that you love doing together, now would be a great time to do it again. Chances are, you'll remember why you two became friends in the first place.

## Leave the Fight in the Past and Move Forward

Now is not the time to hold a grudge, although it can be tempting to bring up the past the next time you and your friend find yourselves in a hot spot. Try and hold back from doing this.

## Remember...

Sometimes you and your friend will find you keep having the same fight over and over again, and this makes it especially hard to keep things in the past. If this happens to you, maybe it's time to take a closer look at the friendship and try to figure out what's at the core of these regular fights.

## The Votes Are In

If you and your friend had a crush on the same person, what would you do?

**Keep it a secret among your friends: 55%**
**Tell him or her to pick one of you: 27%**
Fight over him or her: 18%

## From the Mentors

When I argue with my friends, it's usually just about small things: where to eat, what movie to see, things like that. We usually just solve the problem by compromising, or flipping a coin. When it's all resolved, you have a stronger bond, and it just feels good to not be arguing anymore. **—JARON**

## JOURNAL KICKSTART! When Friends Fight

Want to think deeper and express yourself about this chapter? Open up your journal, write down one or more of these sentence starters, and then see where your words and feelings take you.

- The biggest fight I've ever had with a friend or friends was when...
- My friends and I worked out our biggest fight by...
- When I get into fights with friends, it's usually about...
- To avoid future fights, I think I could be better at...
- To avoid future fights, I think my friend or friends could be better at...

# Special Types of Fights

There are fights, and then there are THESE types of fights, which call for a little extra advice:

**Crushing on the same person:** Ask around, and you'll see that two friends having a crush on the same person is pretty high on everyone's "things-to-fight-about" list. Crushes and friendship are two of the most intense things in our lives. When they crash into each other... BAM! Here are some tips on how to keep that from happening:

## DON'Ts

- Don't go behind your friend's back.
- Don't talk trash about your friend.
- Don't force your crush to choose.

## DO's

- Do talk it over with your friend.
- Do back off if you can.
- Do remember the reasons why you're friends.

**Group fights:** Sometimes a fight between two people is like a snowball rolling downhill. You get one or two friends on your side, and your friend gets one or two friends on his or her side, and suddenly that snowball is getting A LOT bigger. Before you know it... avalanche! What started as a private little issue has evolved into a full-blown group fight. Group fights are incredibly awkward for everyone involved because:

- If you're the one fighting, you suddenly have twice, three times, or even five times as many people mad at you!
- If you're not fighting but are being forced to choose sides, you get stuck in the middle.
- You might find yourself on opposite sides from someone for no good reason.

While you can't control how the friend you're fighting with handles things, you can decide NOT to drag other friends into the middle of your conflict. If friends want to jump in and take sides, don't let them. If you're able to keep other people out of it, you have a better chance of solving the problem quickly, and with as little long-term damage to your group of friends as possible.

**When friends fight dirty:** A small disagreement can turn into an epic fight — or even the end of a friendship — if someone decides to fight dirty. This can include things like: ganging up on you, spreading gossip, or completely ignoring you. If you've tried talking to your friends with no results, it's time to bring in a school counselor or another trusted adult to help sort it all out. Here's what some of you had to say about being ignored by friends and how to deal with it:

## From the Mentors

I've had fights with my friends over girls, and those are usually the worst. Usually what I do to resolve a problem is give my friend and myself some time to cool down. Then I'll approach him or her and try get the other person's point of view, and use that to bring about some sort of resolution. It is usually a long process and takes some time. **—WILLIAM**

*"I tried to talk to him, but he kept walking away. So I left him alone, and started to play with other kids, and he got jealous. Then he wanted to be my friend again."*

**—ROBERTO, 11**

*"I used to have two very good friends, but they started ignoring me and leaving me out. I calmly and patiently talked to them, and told them that I felt like they were leaving me out, and it never happened again."*

**—LINDSEY, 12**

*"My friends ignored me and did some very mean things to me. I just moved on and found new, nicer friends who love me for me. For once, I don't have to try and be someone else!"*

**—KELLY, 13**

*"My friends have felt that I've ignored them sometimes. They came and talked to me about it. Explain how you feel!"*

**—JESS, 13**

## JOURNAL KICKSTART! I-Messages

Ready to practice some I-Messages? Think about something you'd like to express to a friend. On a page in your journal, finish these three parts of the message:

- **I feel...** *(Be specific about your emotions. You can use more than one word.)*
- **When you...** *(Give details of how your friend has acted or what he or she has done.)*
- **Because**... *(Why do you think you feel this way?)*

Now, put the three parts together and write it as one sentence! Read it out loud. How does it sound to you?

# It's Your Turn!

So now that you've read through *our* advice, here's your chance to come up with some words of wisdom of your own! Pretend you're the advice columnist for your school newspaper. Copy down this question in your journal and write a response:

*One of my friends likes to talk about the other. If I don't join in, she'll get mad. The other friend does the same exact thing! I don't want to talk about either friend, what should I do?* —AUTUMN, 10

## From the Mentors

My friends and I usually fight over little things, like one of us forgetting to share a secret we shared with another friend. We've also had really big fights: last year my best friend and I stopped talking to each other and this went on for three months. Eventually, it got too hard NOT to talk to each other. I finally sat down with her and we had what was the start of many conversations trying to patch things up. We became decent friends again, but it's taken a full year for us to get back to full-friend status. Patience really is a virtue. —ELIZABETH

# Quotes From Kids Like You

*"My friends and I fight mostly about boys. Like when my friend said I was flirting with her BF, we solved it by just spending time apart."*

**—MEGAN, 12**

*"I told my friend that I liked a boy, and she said that she liked him too. We got in a BIG fight, and we weren't friends for about 1 ½ months. We finally figured out that he was a jerk, and we were friends again."*

**—JACKIE, 11**

*"I don't fight with my friends, but my friends fight with each other. When they do, I don't pick sides. I just go sit with another group until everything gets back to normal, which is only a day or two!*

**—TIFFANY, 12**

*"I try to find out what happened, or why I got mad, and I try to apologize."*

**—ANN, 12**

*"My friend got mad at me when I played with another friend instead of him. I finally got the courage to tell my friend I'm sorry, and now we're friends again,"*

**—ALEXIS, 11**

# Quiz:
# Do YOU Fight Fair?

**For each question, circle a letter choice, and then see the Answer Key for your results!**

1. Two friends in your group get into a fight, and the insults start to fly. One of the friends involved is your BFF. You...

   **a.** Take your BFF's side and try to get the rest of the group to join forces against the other friend, escalating the fight.
   **b.** Stay out of it, because the fight is between your BFF and the other person. They can work it out on their own.
   **c.** Give the friend your BFF is fighting with the silent treatment. After all, you have to be loyal, right?

2. Your close friend did something to embarrass you, and you've been in a fight ever since. But now that you're over the humiliation, you really wish the two of you could be on good terms again. You...

   **a.** Take the first step and tell your friend you want to make things right, whether it was your fault or not. Saving your friendship is more important than being right.
   **b.** Ask another friend to act as a go-between, and tell the friend you're fighting with that you want to make up if he or she takes the first step.
   **c.** Wait it out. Your friend is the one who started the fight, and he or she should be the one to come to you and apologize first.

3. **After confiding in one of your friends about your crush, suddenly the rest of the group is in on the secret. You're so angry about your loose-lipped friend that you can hardly see straight. You...**

**a.** Confront him or her immediately. It's better to get things off your chest right away so you can cool off afterward.

**b.** Take a step back and think about the situation, trying to see it from all sides before coming up with a plan.

**c.** Blow off some steam by venting to another friend. Then, when you approach the blabbermouth, you won't be so hotheaded.

4. **You and a friend have been fighting for a while now. So long, in fact, that you don't even remember what started the argument in the first place. You've decided to take the first step toward repairing your friendship. You...**

**a.** See your friend online, and decide to make a halfhearted attempt to fix things over the Internet.

**b.** Ask another person to approach your friend on your behalf. Once you know he or she is interested in making up, you can take it from there.

**c.** Plan out what you're going to say, find your friend, and ask for a few minutes to talk. What you need to say should be said in person so there are no misunderstandings.

**5.** After getting the cold shoulder from your friend for a week, you decide to get things out in the open face-to-face. Once you get things off your chest, you...

   **a.** Sit back and give your friend a chance to speak his or her mind, listening without interrupting until he or she has gotten their point across.

   **b.** Listen to what your friend has to say until he or she says something that is totally off the mark. There's no point in continuing until all the facts are straight.

   **c.** Keep talking until you're sure that your friend understands where you're coming from. Making sure he or she hears you out is the most important thing.

**6.** You and your friend aren't seeing eye-to-eye, again. It seems the two of you get into fights just about every other week. But you're not ready to end the friendship, so you...

   **a.** Remind your friend of the last fight you had, which was his or her fault. After all, it's only right to bring up the last time your friend was in the wrong.

   **b.** Treat your friend like this is the first time you've been in a fight. Things that happened in the past should stay there.

   **c.** Try to work things out without bringing up the past, but when your friend drags up old situations, you can't help but do the same.

## Answer Key

Go through and add up the points for each answer you circled:

1. a = 10    b = 0    c = 5      4. a = 5    b = 10    c = 0
2. a = 0    b = 5    c = 10      5. a = 0    b = 5    c = 10
3. a = 10    b = 0    c = 5      6. a = 10    b = 0    c = 5

How many points do you have?

**0 – 20 Points = Turn the Other Cheek**
While all friends fight every now and then, you know that fighting fair is an important part of keeping up healthy relationships. Even when things get tough, you know how to handle them with grace and fairness to make sure your friendships stay solid.

**25 – 45 Points = Pillow Fight**
You try to handle fights with friends as best you can, but every now and then you make choices that might cause more strain than gain. If you're not careful, you might find that some of your techniques have the opposite effect of what you intended.

**45 – 60 Points = Take Off the Boxing Gloves!**
Most of the time it's more important for you to be right than to resolve fights with your friends. If you're not careful, you might be the last one talking… but no one will be around to listen.

# CHAPTER 4

# GOSSIP AND RUMORS

**P**ssssst... did you hear? Gossip and rumors are everywhere. Sometimes it seems like we can barely get through the week without hearing, spreading, or being the subject of something juicy. Maybe you know firsthand how dangerous rumors and gossip can be. If not, hopefully by the time you finish reading this chapter, you'll come to the following conclusion:

## The gossip must STOP!
### (Pass it on.)

# Do you know the difference between
# GOSSIP and a RUMOR?

## rumor (rōōmər) n.
*A piece of unverified information of uncertain origin usually spread by word of mouth.*

The key word here is "unverified" — there's no way to tell if the info being passed around is true or not. Because rumors are spread from person to person, they can change with each retelling. Like the games "telephone" or "whisper down the lane" (in which players whisper the same phrase from person to person in a circle, repeating it based on what they think they've heard), a rumor started in the morning might be completely different by the end of the day. A little exaggeration here, a dab of shock value there, and suddenly the rumor has a life of its own. Rumors can be about completely unbelievable things, but usually the people spreading them don't care if they're true or not. The thrill is in the *telling* of the rumor — that's it. Here's what a rumor might sound like:

*"I heard that Mr. Shaner gives A's to all the basketball players."*

*"Did you hear that the teachers are required by law to flunk 5 percent of their classes each year?"*

Short list for identifying a **rumor:**

- No way to know if it's true or not.
- Spreads from person to person.
- Can be unbelievable.
- People spreading it don't care if it's true or not.

Ever hear of an urban legend? You know, those "myths" that everyone seems to know about (like, a young actor died from mixing Pop Rocks with soda)? They seem pretty "out there," but you can always find someone who swears the story is true. **Urban legends are nothing more than out-of-control rumors.**

## gossip (gässəp) *n.*
*Talk of a personal, sensational, or intimate nature.*

Gossip is usually spread behind someone's back, often started by people who want to make someone else look bad. While rumors can be about anything, gossip tends to hit below the belt — focusing on that personal, sensitive stuff like love, family, and relationships, or other kinds of things that people don't want the whole world knowing. Is gossip true? Sometimes it is, sometimes it isn't. But even if it *is*, it's still hurtful. Check out this example and you'll see what we mean:

> *"Karie said that when Joel tried to kiss her he slobbered all over her face! Gross!"*

Okay, so maybe Joel really does slobber a little. He's probably self-conscious enough as it is without the whole school knowing about his technique!

Short list to identifying gossip:

- It's spread behind someone's back.
- Intention of hurting someone.
- Can be true or false.
- Usually about private and personal stuff.

# Why Gossip and Rumors are Bad News

If you've been the subject of a rumor or gossip, you probably already know why it's so bad. But even when you're not the target, it can still spell trouble for you, because:

- **Words can hurt.** Although you might not bruise, the effect of gossip and rumors can be just as painful. Gossip is actually a form of bullying, which is serious business.
- **Gossip and rumors are a form of exclusion.** If you're the one being gossiped about, you're "out," while the gossipmongers are "in."
- **They can destroy trust.** If you've confided in someone about something, and suddenly your private issue is all over school, chances are you won't trust that friend again.
- **True or not, private is private.** Some people think that if gossip is true, there's no harm done. Wrong!
- **Believing rumors can lead to bad choices.** Usually, there's no way to know if a rumor is true or not, so making decisions based on that information can be a big mistake.

## Remember...

By laughing at or reacting to a rumor in a way that makes it seem like it's okay, you're being part of the problem, NOT the solution.

# Why People Gossip

Gossiping can be hard to avoid, especially among close friends. Most of us can probably recall a time when we've gossiped and didn't even realize that we were doing so. But some people go out of their way to be the ones dishing the dirt. What's in it for them?

- **Superiority**: Making others look bad can make some people feel better about themselves.
- **Inclusion:** Who wants to be left out when everyone else is in on the secret? It's scary to be on the outside, so jumping in on the gossip can make someone feel more included.
- **Attention:** Having a juicy tidbit to share suddenly puts all the attention on you, especially if you build it up among your friends (*"Wait until you hear what I found out about Jamie!"*) It's just like having a great new outfit, gadget, or haircut. Sometimes, people use gossip to get themselves on the good side of a group they want to be part of, especially if it's the "in" crowd.
- **Power**: If someone is on top of the social ladder, he or she might do anything to stay there, including spreading rumors or gossip about someone who might knock them out of position.
- **Jealousy:** People who are jealous of someone's looks or popularity might want to spread gossip about that person to level the playing field.
- **Revenge:** Most gossip is started with the purpose of hurting; it's only natural that someone might be tempted to spread a lie about a certain person to get back at him or her for something.
- **Boredom:** Some people just aren't happy unless there's conflict around them. If everyone is getting along fabulously, these are the kids who might be tempted to stir things up to keep life "exciting."

# Handling Gossip and Rumors

Gossip and rumors get their fuel from us... the people who spread them. Starting a rumor is just like striking a match in a forest full of dry, dead trees. Once the fire gets going, it's nearly impossible to put it out. Since the only person you can control is you, don't throw another log onto the pile. Need help resisting the temptation? When you hear gossip or a rumor, ask yourself these questions:

**1.** Do I want to pass this scoop on for any of these reasons: to feel included, to put someone else down, to feel better about myself? YES / NO

**2.** Would I be upset if this rumor were about *me*? YES / NO

**3.** Would this person be upset if he or she knew this rumor was being spread? YES / NO

**4.** Will this rumor lower this person's status or exclude him or her from the group? YES / NO

If you answered "YES" to any of these questions, then the juicy tidbit you've got isn't one that should be passed along. Instead, take the following action:

**Make the rumor stop with you.** You might think that keeping your lips sealed won't make a difference, but it will. If everyone decided not to pass it on, the flame of the rumor would fizzle out quicker than you can say "fire hose."

**Don't be an audience.** If a friend approaches you just dying to share some big scoop, tell him you don't want to hear it. Not only will you keep your hands clean, but your friend won't get the result — feeling powerful and included — that he's looking for.

**Respect others' privacy.** Remind yourself that another person's privacy, safety, and trust are more important than anything you might gain by passing on a rumor. Respecting another's privacy means he or she will be more likely to do the same for you.

**Get the facts.** If there's a rumor going around that you want to take action on (like this one: *"Teachers aren't allowed to give pop quizzes the day before a school holiday"*), do some fact checking and see if it's true before you do anything (or don't do anything... like study!).

## The Votes Are In
What do you usually do when you hear a juicy rumor?

**Ignore it: 40%**   Pass it along: 19%
**Try to find out if it's true or not: 41%**

## From the Mentors
Sometimes when you get into a fight, it's somewhat "natural" for you to say bad things about the other person. However, after you cool off, you'll usually regret what you've said. But if other people twist your words and spread them around, you just can't stop it. So my advice is to always think before you speak, especially when you want to say something bad about someone else. Just write all the things down and tear up the paper. It will help you release your anger without getting you into trouble. **—JOYCE**

# When the Rumor's About YOU

Being the target of gossip or a rumor can be devastating, horrifying, and just plain terrible. No wonder it's such a common form of bullying, and make no mistake: it IS a form of bullying, one that can happen to anyone. Chances are, if you haven't been already, you'll be the target of gossip at some point. But keep your cool, because being prepared can make all the difference. Follow these steps to handle the rumor mill with grace, and most importantly, always go with your gut. If it's a situation you don't feel comfortable handling on your own, talk to a trusted adult as soon as you can.

- **Understand where it's coming from and why.** Do a little fact checking of your own, and try to find out who started the rumor and why. Was it intentional? Was he or she just joking around? Trying to embarrass you? Get revenge? This is important stuff, and you'll be able to figure out the best way to handle the situation once you know what's behind it.
- **Get someone in the middle to take a stand.** You need friends at a time like this, and finding someone who can help you fizzle out the rumor can be a great way to go. It can be very effective for your peeps to offer up honest and direct responses like, "I know for a fact that's not true," or, "I wouldn't spread something around unless you know what really happened." (*NOTE: This doesn't mean you should force your friends to pick sides resulting in a nasty group fight. You just need a little help in pouring water on the fire.*)

- **Don't give the bully what he or she wants.** This is the most important step, and probably the hardest. Since people who start rumors and gossip about someone else are usually trying to either (1) hurt that person, or (2) make themselves look better, take away their power by STAYING CALM. The gossiper is going for a reaction, so leave her high and dry. Chances are, she'll get bored with you and move on to a new victim.
- **If the rumor's serious, get help from a trusted adult**. What happens if a rumor is so bad or generally nasty (such as, having to do with something sexual or violent) that you just can't handle it yourself? That's when it's time to get someone with authority, such as a school counselor or a teacher you really trust, to help cool things off. Don't be afraid to ask for this kind of help when you need it!
- **Resist the urge to get revenge.** 'Nuff said.

## Did You Know?

Research tells us that **boredom** is the number one reason why young people spread rumors!

## From the Mentors

When I find out someone has been gossiping about me, I try not to get upset and just ignore it. In those cases when it's not enough to deny the rumor, I try to talk to the person responsible. When that's not possible, I think it's best to forget it and trust that your real friends will know the difference between the truth and rumor. If you don't make a big deal about it, everybody else will soon forget about it! **—HYDIE**

# Protect Yourself Against Rumors

Here are a few ways you can lower your chances of being gossiped about in the first place:

- **Be careful with your secrets**. You can't stop people from making stuff up about you, but safeguarding your secrets helps you keep what's private *private*.
- **Use the buddy system**. If you must tell someone your secret, tell one friend who you trust, preferably someone who confides in you, too.
- **Resist the urge to dish it out**. Don't give in to gossiping or spreading rumors. If you do, others might decide to give you a taste of your own medicine.

## The Votes Are In

What would you do about a false rumor that was about you?

**Tell everyone it's not true: 50%**
**Ignore it and hope it goes away: 28%**
Find out who started it: 22%

# Quotes From Kids Like You

*"**Once a girl who I was sort of friends with told another friend that I didn't like her.** That friend told me and I decided NEVER to tell the other girl any secrets EVER because she doesn't even need a true secret to spread it."*

**—TALIA, 10**

*"**People spread rumors about me a lot.** I can never figure out why. I just ignore them because I know if I try and stick up for myself, they think I'm lying. I know what's true so it doesn't matter what others say or think."*

**—JILLIAN, 13**

*"**I've been in a billion school rumors and I NEVER got hurt.** Here's how I did it: People would say, 'Hey Krystal, I heard Sam (the cutest boy in school) dumped you last night.' I'd reply, 'Girls! I'm the toughest girl in the 5th grade! If anybody dumped me I'd kick their butts!' Then I'd walk away happily."*

**—KRYSTAL, 10**

*"**I have never been the victim of a rumor but I have started one.** My friend told me who she liked and I told my neighbor. Luckily nobody found out. Then my other friend started teasing me about who I liked. Now I know how she felt and I will never say anything ever again!"*

**—ANONYMOUS**

## From the Mentors

I've been the center of a rumor before and to tell you the truth, it was like living in a nightmare. I was really scared. The best way to deal with it is to ignore the mean remarks, try to get the story straight, and stop it at the source. **—APRIL**

*"Rumors can be hurtful and a source of cruelness. I think gossip is just a way for popular kids to fit in."*

**—KATE, 13**

*"When I was in 5th grade, this girl who was jealous of me spread lots of rumors about me. Since she was popular and everyone wanted to be on her good side, they all excluded me and I was a loner. **I was too shy to defend myself or tell someone, so it just kept getting worse and worse.** Finally, I told my dad and he went down to talk to the principal."*

**—SARAH, 13**

## The Votes Are In

What is your attitude about gossip?

**It's very harmful to people
and relationships: 78%**
**It probably hurts, but not much: 12%**
It's mostly harmless: 10%

## From the Mentors

I think a rumor is harmless when it glorifies or exaggerates something good a person might have done. A rumor becomes ugly, on the other hand, when it hurts feelings or the image of the person the rumor is about. When someone is spreading rumors about me, I try to find out who started them, and why. If it's a really outlandish rumor, I usually don't care, because not too many people will believe it anyway. **—TIFFANY**

# It's Your Turn!

So now that you've read through *our* advice, here's your chance to come up with some words of wisdom of your own! Pretend you're the advice columnist for your school newspaper. Copy down this question in your journal and write a response:

*I was new at the beginning of fifth grade and I wasn't popular, but soon enough I found some friends who wanted to hang out with me. Every day at recess, my friends and I (we're the "cool" group) get together and talk, gossip, and make fun of the "uncool" people. I don't like being a part of this because I know what that's like and how much it hurts. But when I don't join in, my friends say they won't hang out with me anymore. I don't know what to do!* — **ROXANNE, 10**

## JOURNAL KICKSTART! Gossip & Rumors

Want to think deeper and express yourself about this chapter? Open up your journal, write down one or more of these sentence starters, and then see where your words and feelings take you.

- The most hurtful rumor I ever heard was...
- I think the most common reason kids spread gossip and rumors is...
- One rumor or piece of gossip I've heard people say about me is...
- This made me feel...
- If I hear one person spreading rumors or lies about another I would...

# How Do You Deal with Gossip and Rumors?

**For each question, circle a letter choice, and then see the Answer Key for your results!**

1. You meet up with your friends in the cafeteria on the first day of school only to find they're all talking about the same thing: Haley's outfit. There's a rumor going around that it's actually a costume from the drama department, and she's wearing it because her family can't afford new back-to-school clothes! You...

   **a.** Stand up for Haley and tell your friends that you think she's a unique trendsetter, ending the discussion there.
   **b.** Don't want to feel left out of the conversation, so you join in on the fun. After all, it's just a harmless little rumor!
   **c.** Can't help but laugh at your friends' biting comments, even though you feel a little bad about making fun of someone.

2. Your BFF was the target of a nasty rumor, and you just found out that Kevin was the one who started spreading it around. You also just overheard your parents talking about Kevin's father getting fired from his job. You...

**a.** Decide it's payback time because he started the rumor about your BFF. Now he can find out what it feels like to be the target of gossip.

**b.** Tell your BFF what you found out. It makes you both feel a little better to know that Kevin's going through some rough times of his own.

**c.** Don't do anything about this new info. You know how much that rumor hurt your BFF. If you try to get revenge by starting more gossip, when will the cycle end? You figure, the best way to stand up for your friend is to talk to Kevin and ask him to stop spreading the rumor.

3. Jessie only made the soccer team because her dad offered to pay for everyone's equipment this year. You know this is true because you heard the soccer coach explaining it to another parent. Meanwhile, your sister, who is a much better player, was cut from the team. You...

**a.** Tell your close friends what you found out, after swearing them to secrecy. This is one bit of news you just can't keep to yourself.

**b.** Decide to keep your mouth shut. After all, gossip is gossip, whether it's true or not. If you were in Jessie's shoes, you would be horrified if the whole school knew the truth.

**c.** Start a petition to have Jessie removed from the team. It's just not fair that she gets to play while better players don't.

4. You just uncovered some serious scoop about Christina, one of the most popular girls in school. You know the dirt could get you in with another group of kids you've been dying to befriend. You...

**a.** Rush over and spill the beans to the group, loving the attention they pour on you.

**b.** Use the fact that you know the scoop to get on the group's good side, without ever having to actually spread the rumor.

**c.** Keep the tidbit to yourself, and try and find other ways to connect with the group you want to get in with. If they only like you for your info, chances are they won't stick around once they know the dirt.

5. **There's a rumor going around that school will close early on Friday. You're psyched because you're supposed to have a history test that afternoon, but if school closes early, you're off the hook! You...**

**a.** Keep your fingers crossed that the rumor is the real thing, but study anyway — just in case.

**b.** Pass the rumor along. Hey, if enough people believe it, maybe the school will be forced to close early either way!

**c.** Go to the school office and find out if there's any truth behind the rumor. If there isn't, you and your friends need to be prepared for the big exam.

6. **Taylor seems to get attention from everyone, including the person you're crushing on big time. If only they all knew what you knew — that Taylor's really a two-timing cheater! You...**

**a.** Decide to keep the information to yourself. Your crush will find out the truth about Taylor soon enough, and you can keep your hands clean.

**b.** Make little side comments to your crush whenever you have a chance. Even if you don't come right out and say it, hopefully he or she will get the picture.

**c.** Tell your crush what you know. After all, if everyone knew what Taylor was really like, chances are people wouldn't be so interested in this big faker anymore.

## Answer Key

Go through and add up the points for each answer you circled:

1. a) 0     b) 10     c) 5
2. a) 10     b) 5     c) 0
3. a) 5     b) 0     c) 10
4. a) 10     b) 5     c) 0
5. a) 5     b) 10     c) 0
6. a) 0     b) 5     c) 10

How many points do you have?

### 0 – 20 Points = Dirt Deflector
You handle gossip and rumors with class, knowing that dishing dirt isn't good for anybody involved. Even when sitting by and letting the gossip fly around you seems like the easy thing to do, you tend to stand up and just say no! In the long run, you'll reduce your chances of being the target of a rumor yourself, and earn the trust and respect of those around you.

### 25 – 45 Points = Muddy Waters
While you try to do the right thing, every now and then you find yourself caught in the middle of gossip or a rumor, and aren't quite sure how to handle it. Sometimes you may be part of keeping a rumor alive without even realizing it. By not speaking out against gossip or rumors, you may be sending the signal that it's okay.

### 50 – 60 Points = Full-Fledged Gossipmonger
You get caught up in the spreading of juicy rumors like pouring fuel on a fire. You love being the center of attention, especially when you're surrounded by people dying to hear the latest scoop. Because you're so quick to talk about others, don't be surprised if you find yourself on the other end of a nasty rumor. You'll find out pretty quickly that it's not so much fun!

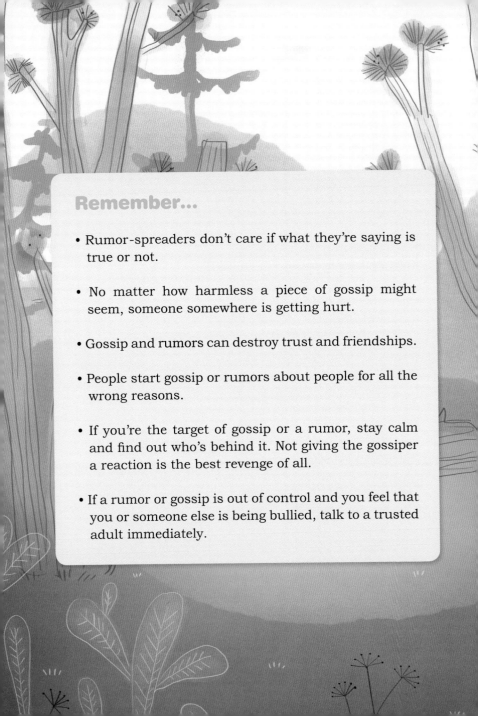

## Remember...

- Rumor-spreaders don't care if what they're saying is true or not.

- No matter how harmless a piece of gossip might seem, someone somewhere is getting hurt.

- Gossip and rumors can destroy trust and friendships.

- People start gossip or rumors about people for all the wrong reasons.

- If you're the target of gossip or a rumor, stay calm and find out who's behind it. Not giving the gossiper a reaction is the best revenge of all.

- If a rumor or gossip is out of control and you feel that you or someone else is being bullied, talk to a trusted adult immediately.

# CHAPTER 5

# HELPING A FRIEND

Everyone goes through hard times. Say your parents are getting divorced, or your grandmother just died. Or maybe you're just having a really rough week at school and you need a shoulder to cry on. When life throws you these curveballs, friends matter more than ever. Think back to a particularly difficult time you've gone through. Did you have a friend to lean on? When a close friend is in bad shape, it can leave us feeling helpless, confused, and clueless. You want to help, but sometimes it's hard to know what exactly to do.

Helping a friend who's hurting isn't always as simple as whipping up a fresh batch of chicken soup or Rice Krispie Treats. Everybody responds to hardship differently, and no two situations are ever the same. What might work for one friend might not be the right way to help another.

# Identifying the Problem

If your friend doesn't come right out and tell you, it's not always easy to know when a friend is going through a rough time. Here are some signs that something might be going on with your friend:

- **Hibernation**: Is your friend hiding out in his or her bedroom or house and only coming up for air when forced?
- **Missing in Action**: Has your friend stopped returning your phone calls?
- **Cling City**: Is your friend being super-clingy or extra-demanding of you and your time?
- **Self-censorship**: Is your friend acting like everything's just fine and dandy, even though you know something big is going down in his or her personal life?
- **Moody**: Is your friend moodier than usual, picking fights with you or just not acting like him- or herself?

If any of these signs sound familiar, or if you just know in your gut that something is "off," check in with your friend and ask what's going on. Even if your friend isn't ready to share all the gory details, he or she will probably appreciate the fact that you noticed something was up and cared enough to ask. Sometimes the worst thing about going through a tough time is feeling like you're all alone.

# Asking the Right Question

So, how do you know what to do for a friend, especially if he or she is completely shutting you out? Just ask this one simple question:

**What's your intention?** If you're going out on a limb for a friend in need, take a step back and question your *motivation*. Are you helping your friend so he or she likes you better? Are you helping your friend because you feel you're expected to do so? Or are you helping your friend because you really, truly want to ease his or her pain? If your intention isn't good, the chances are that the outcome won't be what you want.

You might be surprised at the answer you get. Maybe all your friend needs is some good hanging-out time with you, where you don't talk about "the problem" at all. Maybe he wants some alone time. Maybe she wants to have a heart-to-heart. The most important part of asking that question is listening to the answer. By asking this question, you're throwing the ball into your friend's court. It says to your friend, "All I really want to do is be there for you, in the best way I can, but I need a little help getting pointed in the right direction."

# Providing the Right Kind of Help

Here are just some of the ways a good friend might be able to help a friend through a rough time:

- Leaning over and sharing your shoulder (everyone needs one to cry on now and then).
- **Listening** to your friend's thoughts and feelings.
- **Supporting** your friend however he or she needs it.
- **Understanding** that your friend is in a difficult situation.
- **Providing distractions** for your friend.
- **Empathizing:** To empathize means to put yourself in someone else's shoes. This is a great thing to do when a friend is hurting. If you're able to see the situation from his or her point of view, it might make you better able to help.
- Most of all, be flexible and forgiving. If your friend is going through something really tough, he or she just might not be the same old reliable friend you're used to. As much as you can, try to give your friend a break. Things will get back to normal when he or she is feeling better.

## The Votes Are In

What's the best way to help a friend who's feeling down?

**Offer to listen if she needs to talk: 62%**
**Surprise her with something fun: 31%**
Send her a card or letter: 7%

# When You're the One Who Needs Help

Sometimes, lending a hand or listening ear is easy... but asking for these things is hard. Maybe you don't want to admit you need help, or you're afraid of being "a pain." First, keep this in mind: as eager as you are to help your friends, your friends are probably just as eager to help you. Helping feels good, right? So, give your friends a chance to feel good.

If you're having trouble communicating your S.O.S., and even a written message like "I need someone to talk to" or "I'm feeling down, can you come cheer me up?" feels awkward, try less obvious tactics. Invite a friend to an activity you know will make you feel better — coming over to watch your favorite movie, for instance, or going for a walk. You don't have to say why, but you may find that once you're together, you're better able to express your feelings and needs.

## Remember...

When someone you care about is hurting, it's normal to try to make the person feel better by saying things like, "It'll be okay," or, "You're going to be fine." In reality, such comments can make the person feel awkward and misunderstood. If your friend is going through a lot of pain, you have to accept that you cannot make that pain go away.

## Thinking Outside the Box...
## Creative Ways to Help a Friend:

- Make a coupon book for your friend with coupons she can redeem whenever she wants. Here are some ideas for what the coupons could be worth: one trip to his favorite spot for quality hang time; one sleepover where the "situation" isn't discussed; one venting session (your friend gets to vent, you get to listen) and so on. You get the point!
- Give a homemade or store-bought card that tells your friend you're thinking of him or her.
- Surprise your friend with something he or she loves. For instance, tickets to Six Flags, homemade brownies, or a movie night with a big bag of popcorn.

## From the Mentors

Whenever my friends are sick, I try to make them feel better. One time I made a GIANT card for a friend, then walked to her house. I knocked on her door, handed it to her, smiled, and walked away. Show your friends that you care. The more you appreciate them, the more they will appreciate you. So when they're sick, call and check up, or if you can, BRING CHICKEN SOUP!! **—JESSICA**

The best thing about a friend is that she or he is always there for you. When my great-grandparents died, my best friends came over and let me just cry on their shoulders. And when my friends have had troubles, I'm always on the phone or at their house comforting them the whole time. **—DANIELLE**

# Quotes From Kids Like You

"I wanted to help my friend when her parents were getting divorced, but unfortunately when I found out, they were already divorced. I feel bad that I didn't help her out or anything."

**—RACHEL, 12**

"This is not really personal but I had a boyfriend who was really cute and I honestly thought that we were going to be together for a long time, but he dumped me. I felt really sad but I didn't show it around him. My best friend Brittany let me talk to her about it and she was just there for me 100%"

**—PARIS, 11**

"When my dog died, I was really sad. Part of the reason I got over it was because my best friend Allison was really nice and there for me. She even made me a 'Feel Better' card!"

**—JILLY, 12**

"I was there for my friend when her brother tried to commit suicide and was in the hospital for depression. I was there when her parents split up and when her grandfather died. I think it's very important to show how much you care and always be there for your friends!"

**—KAT, 13**

*"I was helped by one of my closest friends when my aunt died and then my best friend died two months later. Now I know I can help people in need of help."*

**—MONIES**

**"Who hasn't been in a difficult situation?** *I mean... come on. I don't know about anyone else, but problems come by every day for me. That's what friends are for, helping you through that stuff. I've been through endless bad situations and so have my friends, and we all just help each other get through them."*

**—SERAH**

## From the Mentors

When I got sick at age 13, it was the friends I made at sick kids' camp and online through a website for sick kids that I was able to "adjust" to a new lifestyle. I had serious responsibilities and if I did not take care of myself, I could die. But with the support of my friends, I learned how to take care of myself. That was several years ago, but it is still my friends that keep me going. **—LEAH**

I've been helped by friends and helped friends many times. When you pull through the problems, it feels great to have someone there with you, because through those experiences you grow closer to them and become better friends. **—JARON**

# It's Your Turn!

So now that you've read through our advice, here's your chance to come up with some words of wisdom of your own! Pretend you're the advice columnist for your school newspaper. Copy down this question in your journal and write a response:

*My friend's dad just passed away. She's very upset and isn't returning my phone calls or talking to me. I don't know what to do to help her.* — **NIKKI, 12**

**JOURNAL KICKSTART!**

## Helping a Friend

Want to think deeper and express yourself about this chapter? Open up your journal, write down one or more of these sentence starters, and then see where your words and feelings take you.

- One time when a friend helped me through a tough situation was...
- My friend helped me by...
- If a friend were going through a difficult time, one way I could help is...
- I could ask a friend if he or she needs help by...
- A friend's help is special because...

# What Would You Do?

Read this story and answer the questions at the end. You can also read it with a friend, and then see how each of you answer. Would you handle things the same way?

Emily and Kara are BFFs, and have been for the past three years. They're so close that people have nicknamed them "The Twins." Not only do they look alike, dress alike, and act alike, but they can practically finish each other's sentences. They both feel so lucky to have found such close friends in each other.

Then out of the blue, Emily begins acting differently. It all starts with an unreturned phone call. Kara really needed to check in with Emily about something that just happened with her crush, and couldn't believe that Emily didn't call her back. Kara just shrugs it off, figuring maybe Emily just didn't get her message. Her mom did sound kind of frazzled when she called.

But the weirdness doesn't stop there. Kara notices that lots of their plans start falling through the cracks, like plans to go the movies and their regular nightly catch-up calls. Kara starts to think that she's getting the big Blow Off.

Kara can't help but feel angry. What could she have done to deserve getting treated like this? That's not what friendships are all about! Finally, Kara can't take it anymore and she confronts Emily, demanding to know why she's throwing their friendship down the toilet. She's in for the surprise of her life when Emily breaks down in tears and tells her that her parents are getting a divorce, and she's been a wreck over it.

Now Kara feels terrible... how could she have missed the signs? She decides to make things right. She tries everything: calling her friend every night to check up on her, baking Emily her favorite homemade brownies, even lending Emily a pair of jeans that she absolutely loves. Nothing seems to work. Emily is still as distant as ever. Kara is about to give up on Emily and their friendship. As a last resort, she turns to her mom in tears, asking her what to do. The advice her mom gives her seems so simple, but she decides to give it a shot anyway. It just might work!

The next day at school, Kara pulls Emily aside and tells her how much she wants to help her BFF through the divorce. Then she asks Emily one simple question: "What can I do to help you?"

Emily turns to her friend and smiles, relieved that Kara understands. More than anything, Emily wants to come over to Kara's and hang out, watch movies, and *not* discuss the whole divorce thing. Kara hugs her friend and laughs, wondering why she didn't just ask Emily what she wanted in the first place! Next time her friend is in need of help, she'll know what to do!

**1. Was Emily wrong to not tell Kara what was going on with her when the divorce first started?**

**a.** Yes. Best friends are supposed to share everything, and keeping her in the dark wasn't fair to their friendship.

**b.** No. Emily was going through something tough and had a right to her privacy.

**c.** Maybe. It could have been helpful to have Kara in the loop from the very start, but it was up to Emily to share it or not.

_____ says (circle one):     **a**      **b**      **c**

_____ says (circle one):     **a**      **b**      **c**

**2. Did Kara have a right to be mad at Emily for blowing her off, even after she found out about the divorce?**

**a.** Yes. Even though Emily was going through something tough, that doesn't mean that you can treat your friends like dirt.

**b.** No. Real friends would give each other a break, especially when dealing with something as difficult as a divorce.

**c.** It would be understandable if Kara's feelings were hurt... after all, Emily did check out of their friendship. But now that she knows what was really happening, it should be easier for her to let go of her anger.

_____ says (circle one):     **a**        **b**        **c**

_____ says (circle one):     **a**        **b**        **c**

**3. Should Emily have been more appreciative of Kara's early attempts to cheer her up (such as asking her to the movies and checking in with regular phone calls)?**

**a.** Yes. She should have realized that Kara was making a big effort, even if it wasn't exactly the kind of support that Emily needed.

**b.** No. Because of the tough situation Emily was going through, she can't be expected to be a perfect friend right now.

**c.** Maybe... even if the help Kara was offering wasn't exactly what she needed just then, she could have realized that Kara was doing the best she could do.

_____ says (circle one):     **a**        **b**        **c**

_____ says (circle one):     **a**        **b**        **c**

**4.** How would you have handled the situation if you were in Kara's shoes?

   **a.** Just like Kara, I would have done everything I could think of to cheer Emily up.

   **b.** I would have confronted Emily much earlier and asked her what was going on as soon as I knew something was "off."

   **c.** I would have backed off and given Emily space to go deal with the divorce. The last thing she needs right now is a demanding BFF.

_____ says (circle one):   **a**    **b**    **c**

_____ says (circle one):   **a**    **b**    **c**

### Remember...

- To ask your friend what he or she needs from you, and listen to the answer.

- That sometimes just letting your friend know you're there for him or her is all it takes.

- To be flexible and forgiving when your friend is going through a rough time.

# CHAPTER 6

# OPPOSITE-SEX FRIENDSHIPS

Okay, here's the gazillion dollar question:

## Can boys and girls really, truly be friends with each other?

If you've lost sleep over this one, you're not alone. In fact, movies, books, and TV shows are constantly exploring this age-old issue. The answer? Well, what do you think?

*"I have had a few friends who are boys and I have to say it was pretty cool. I like having a person to talk to who won't turn on me if I say the wrong thing. It's great just to hang out and not worry if they like you or not."*

**—KATE, 13**

*"I have had a friend that was the opposite sex and it's okay, but then it got harder because I started to like him."*

**—ABIGAIL, 11**

As you can see, in many ways the answer is up to you. Let's go back to square one and revisit the definition of "friendship" that we came up with earlier:

**Friends are people who make you feel good about yourself, people you can really be yourself around, and people who will tell you if you have a big hunk of spinach in your teeth.**

Seems simple enough, right? And there's nothing in there that says friends have to be the same sex as you are. It really *is* up to you and your friend to define the relationship. But it's not always that easy, as you probably know. Maybe nobody cared whether you were best friends with boys or girls in kindergarten or even second grade, so why does it have to be complicated now? That's because when you hit the preteen years, two things happen at once:

- The idea of "romance" may no longer seem totally gross.
- People around you — your peers as well as adults — have more expectations about the ways in which boys and girls should act differently... and how they should act *together*.

In other words...

# One of you might develop
# a CRUSH on the other.

Yowza! This doesn't have to happen, of course. But it's possible that at some point one of you will suddenly realize that this friend, who may know your secrets and dreams, has seen you at your best and worst, is someone you want to be with in a romantic way. After all, you're already close on so many other levels. Why not just become a "couple"? If the crush thing happens, there are a several possible outcomes:

1. Your friend crushes on you, but you don't feel the same. The dynamic in your relationship is changed, and you'll forever wonder if your friend still has a crush on you. Everything is totally ruined.
2. You crush on your friend, but he or she doesn't feel the same. Same as above. Everything is totally ruined.
3. You both crush on each other at the same time! Yahoo! But after you become a couple, it doesn't really work out, and you break up. You can't get the friendship back now. Everything is totally ruined.
4. One of you crushes on the other, or you both crush on each other. Maybe it will always be a little weird, maybe you'll go out with each other for a week or a month or a year or more. But whatever happens, you are strong enough friends to work things out. You fight to save the friendship and it survives. Everything is totally cool.

Still confused? Don't worry — we all are. People have been pondering the question of opposite-sex friendships for years, and that's because there are no easy answers. Even though it might seem like opposite-sex friendships are more complicated than others, they're also worth fighting for.

# The Benefits of Opposite-Sex Friendships

If you've got a close friend of the opposite sex, you know that there are some awesome benefits to hanging out with people from "the other side," such as:

**Gaining insight:** Having a friend of the opposite sex takes some of the guesswork out of day-to-day situations that come up. Not sure how boys *really* feel about girls who wear makeup? Ask your "boy" friend. Curious about whether girls are more attracted to guys who are buff and tough, or smart and funny? Get the real scoop from your "girl" friend. Having a friend of the opposite sex to fill you in on the in's and out's of being who they are can save you lots of frustration and confusion.

**Getting advice from a different perspective:** No matter what you're going through — a tough situation at home, a breakup with a crush at school, being the victim of vicious gossip — sometimes it can be refreshing to get advice from someone who sees the world differently than you do. Often times, friends of the opposite sex can shed a little light on a situation and give you another way to handle what's going on.

**Enjoying different experiences:** Hanging out with same-sex friends can be great; you can bond over movie star crushes or shooting hoops at the park. But these friendships can also have their own baggage: jealousies, petty competitions, and so on.

Chances are, when you and your opposite-sex friend hang out, it's much different than your other relationships. Breaking out of that routine can be a breath of fresh air. In fact, sometimes opposite-sex friendships can be less work than same-sex ones because the expectations are different. You might even find you can be yourself in a way you can't be with your usual group.

## The Votes Are In

Do you think boys and girls can truly be friends?

**Yes, of course: 21%**
**No, someone always gets a crush: 61%**
Sometimes, if you work on it: 18%

## Wait. What About Crushes On Same-Sex Friends?

Of course, it happens. It's *extra* confusing, yes, and probably *extra* terrifying to think about revealing your feelings. The fallout of rejection can be *extra* awkward, too. Even if the crush feelings are mutual, you and your friend might not be able to become a public couple as easily as an opposite-sex pair would. This is where walking the line between a close friendship and a crush gets really tricky and possibly painful. Know that all this is normal, and do what you believe is best for both you and your friend... whatever that may be.

# The Obstacles to Opposite-Sex Friendships

All right, having friends of the opposite sex can be a terrific thing. So, what's the problem? Here are some of the obstacles you and your opposite-sex friend might find yourself up against:

**The parent trap:** Many parents just don't "get" the idea that boys and girls can be friends with each other. Sometimes when kids reach a certain age, parents assume that all girls are boy-crazy and vice versa. Suspicious parents might not believe you when you insist, "We're only friends!" This misinterpreting of your relationship can get pretty annoying.

**Clueless friends:** Many same-sex friends aren't any better than parents. That is, if you're spending lots of time with a friend of the opposite sex, your friends and other kids at school are bound to start thinking something's up. While this doesn't change your relationship with your friend, it can make it a little uncomfortable for you both, especially if your peers decide to tease you and make your life miserable.

**Labels and stereotypes:** There will always be people who believe girls should spend most of their time with other girls, and boys with other boys. They might raise an eyebrow if it's otherwise and make assumptions about your sexual orientation. Whether the assumption is true or not, it's a bummer when someone can't look past all that to see friendship for what it is: friendship.

**Mixed signals**: One of the most challenging aspects about having a friend of the opposite sex is that things can get confusing really quickly. You might find yourself analyzing everything your friend does a little differently than you would with your same-sex friends:

- He's acting more jokey and chummy lately. Is he flirting, or just trying to become better friends?
- If she calls you more than usual, does that mean she "likes" you?
- If he asks you to dance at a social event, has the friendship turned into more?
- Are opposite-sex friends allowed to touch each other — hugging, arms around the shoulder, cheek-kissing — the way same-sex friends do?

# It's Your Turn!

So now that you've read through our advice, here's your chance to come up with some words of wisdom of your own! Pretend you're the advice columnist for your school newspaper. Copy down this question in your journal and write a response:

*My BGF (best guy friend) is really nice online and when we are alone.* **I really like him as a friend, but I don't like it that he acts different when we are around other people.** *He tries to act cool and disses me. He does this to my other friends, too. I tried talking to him about it, but it didn't really sink in. That's the way he is. What should I do?* — **CARRIE, 13**

# The Ground Rules

What are the rules? Unfortunately, there are no easy answers here. It's different for everyone, so it's up to you and your friend to figure out what you're comfortable with. Even so, things can still get confusing, particularly when it comes to...

**Unexpected crushes:** Ah... the biggest obstacle of them all. Even if you've been friends with your opposite-sex friend since the day you both ran around naked in the backyard as toddlers, there's always the chance that one day, something in one of you will "click." You might suddenly look at your friend and realize that he's the boy of your dreams. Or maybe your buddy's annoying giggle one day seems like the cutest sound you've ever heard. In a split second, your friendship can turn into a major crush. The history you have together can make these types of crushes even more mixed-up than the regular kind.

So, Where Does That Leave Us? Right back where we started. Opposite-sex friendships are common and doable. There are some great bonuses to having friends of the opposite sex in your inner circle. Even when you're facing some tough challenges, don't give up hope. Follow these ground rules, and you'll have a better shot at making it succeed. Hey, all friendships are work, right? Opposite-sex friendships are no exception.

- Don't make decisions about your friendship based on what other people say, do, or think about it.
- Treat your opposite-sex friend with the same respect you would your other friends.

- Appreciate your relationship for the things that make it different from your same-sex friendships.
- If things start to get confusing, remember what qualities you enjoy in your friend (like loyalty, trust, and honesty) and focus on those.

## Quotes From Kids Like You

*I have MANY male friends and they are all very nice. Even though there are rumors about us being b/f g/f, we don't care because the truth is that we are just friends. Friends are friends no matter their color, size, shape, race, whatever.*

**—ACURA, 12**

*"I have so many friends of both sexes. Boys and girls! I like having both kinds of friends because it is fun to see boys' and girls' points of view."*

**—JAIMIE, 12**

**JOURNAL KICKSTART!** **Opposite-Sex Friends**

Want to think deeper and express yourself about this chapter? Open up your journal, write down one or more of these sentence starters, and then see where your words and feelings take you.

- I have had an opposite-sex friendship with…
- The best thing about having friends of the opposite sex is…
- The most challenging thing about having friends of the opposite sex is…
- If a friend told me that he or she had a crush on me, I would…

# What Would You Do?

Read this tale about the challenges of opposite-sex friendships and answer the questions at the end. Or, you can read this with a friend and answer the questions together! Do you see things eye to eye?

Troy and Hannah have been close friends for as long as they can both remember. Ever since Troy's family moved to Hannah's neighborhood back when he was in kindergarten, the two have spent summers and hours after school hanging out, playing games, riding bikes, and exploring.

Now that they're in sixth grade, Hannah especially enjoys their special relationship. After all, Troy gives Hannah great insight into what boys her age are really like, and in return, Hannah gives Troy good advice on how to handle tough situations at home and in school.

But suddenly, the two friends are finding new challenges to deal with. First off, it seems like both of their parents are looking at their friendship differently and coming up with weird rules, like they can't hang out in each others' bedrooms anymore. But that's not the worst of it. Hannah's girlfriends at school have started teasing the two of them about their closeness and hinting that they're really much more than friends.

While she used to just ignore these kinds of comments, Hannah has to admit that she's looking at their relationship a little differently now, too. In fact, she could swear that Troy blushes when he looks at her for too long. And he sounded kind of nervous when he called her the other day and asked her to hang out. Could Troy have a crush on Hannah?

Between the mixed signals she's getting from Troy, and the teasing from her friends, and the weird rules from her parents, Hannah decides to back off from her close relationship with Troy. Right now it just seems like too much to deal with. Besides, she figures that being playmates in elementary school was fine, but now that they're in middle school, the rules are different.

Day by day, Hannah distances herself from Troy. By the end of their first year of middle school, Troy and Hannah are just school buddies who say "hi" in the hallways and that's about it. While Hannah misses parts of their friendship, she just feels it is easier this way.

**1. Did Hannah do the right thing by backing off of her relationship with Troy?**

   **a.** Yes. Opposite-sex friendships get too complicated after a while.
   **b.** No. They had a longtime friendship that was worth hanging onto.
   **c.** Maybe. It depends on whether Troy really did have a crush on Hannah or not.

_____ says (circle one):  **a**  **b**  **c**

_____ says (circle one):  **a**  **b**  **c**

**2. Do you think Troy and Hannah should have stood up to their friends and parents and let them know that they're *just friends*?**

**a.** Yes. Maybe everyone would have backed off then and their friendship could have survived.

**b.** No. Their relationship and what it means to them is no one else's business.

**c.** It wouldn't have made a difference. People will think what they want, and there's no way to control that.

_____ says (circle one):     **a**     **b**     **c**

_____ says (circle one):     **a**     **b**     **c**

**3. Suppose Troy *did* have a crush on Hannah. Do you think this is good cause for ending a friendship?**

**a.** Yes. When friends crush on friends, it never works out well in the end.

**b.** No. True friendships can endure anything, even crushes gone wrong.

**c.** It's tough to say. Depending on whether or not Hannah feels the same way, the relationship might never be the same again.

_____ says (circle one):     **a**     **b**     **c**

_____ says (circle one):     **a**     **b**     **c**

**4. What would you do if you were in Hannah's shoes?**

   **a.** I would have done the same thing as Hannah and ended the close friendship.

   **b.** I would have ignored the teasing and remembered what Troy's friendship meant to me in the first place.

   **c.** I'm not sure. Opposite-sex friendships are definitely challenging and this situation is a tough one.

_____ says (circle one):   **a**    **b**    **c**

_____ says (circle one):   **a**    **b**    **c**

## Remember...

- Your opposite-sex friendship is between you and your friend... try to ignore any gossip that might get in the way.

- Opposite-sex friendships can offer great insight and solid advice from a completely different perspective.

- Friendships that turn into crushes are completely normal, and it doesn't have to mean the end of your relationship.

# CHAPTER 7

# LONG-DISTANCE FRIENDSHIPS

## It just plain stinks!

Maybe you're moving to a new city, or you just found out your BFF's father has been transferred to another state.

Or maybe you've just met an awesome friend at summer camp, but she lives halfway across the country.

The bad news is, you and your compadre may never have that day-to-day, in-person relationship again. The good news is, you can still have a strong long-distance connection that might bring unexpected bonuses... if you're willing to help make it work.

# How to Deal

There's no doubt about it: when a friend moves away or you're the one moving, it can suddenly feel like there's a big hole in your life. You might even feel something similar to grief, and that's totally natural and normal. When you can't shake the sadness at not having your friend around every day, here are some things to remember:

- Your friendship is not ending — it is just changing.
- Keep yourself open to closer relationships with existing friends, or maybe to somebody completely new.
- Keep a journal or express yourself in some other way, like painting, drawing, or writing poetry.
- Stay involved in the sports, hobbies, and other activities you really enjoy.
- Don't keep your feelings bottled up. If you need to get something off your chest, talk to a parent, sibling, or school counselor.

## From the Mentors

What you'll miss most after leaving a summer camp is the friendships you formed. What I do is send e-mails from time to time updating them on what's happening around me and stuff like that. I think it's really important to remember your friends' birthdays and send them a card — by mail, not e-mail — telling them that you remember and that you really want to keep in touch. —**JOYCE**

# Saying Goodbye

**Still bumming? Think about these suggestions for making your farewells easier to deal with:**

**Have a party:** Throw a goodbye party to celebrate your friendship or friendships. Have a shindig at your home or a friend's, or head out to a local park or sporting event. Don't forget to take LOTS of pictures and videos!

**Give a gift:** We give gifts at birthdays and major holidays, so why not give a goodbye gift to a special friend? Find something that has some connection to the things you like to do together, or better yet, make something that's one-of-a-kind. Think about how to show your friend that although you may be far away physically, in your heart you're right next door.

**Make a friendship book:** Alone or together with your friend, make a scrapbook that celebrates your time as friends. Include anything you want, such as: photos, drawings, magazine cutouts, stubs of movies you saw together, or lyrics to your favorite songs. You might want to create two scrapbooks, so that you can each have one when you're separated. Or you could suggest that your friend make a scrapbook to give to you, and you make one to give to him or her.

## From the Mentors

My very best friend is moving away and we tell each other everything. It's going to be really hard to see her go but I'm making her a scrapbook and a 'survival bag' full of stuff she can look at and do if she starts missing us. We're going to stay in contact but we both know it won't be the same. **—LISA**

# So, What's the Upside?

Now that you've learned to cope with thing and said goodbye, it's time to think positive!

## Friends in Faraway Places

How cool is it to have friends in different cities, or maybe even countries? Consider this:

- You can learn firsthand, through your friend, about this new city or region — its history, culture, and geography. You have a connection to it now, which will make it a lot more interesting.
- Arrange for you and your friend to exchange photos of local sights or souvenirs from the area.
- Here's your chance to see how people are different, as well as how they're the same, from place to place. Ask your friend to report back on what's popular in entertainment and sports, common views on politics and social issues, and even what kind of slang is currently trending over there.
- Just imagine the vacation possibilities… New York City during spring break, San Diego in the summer, maybe even an outing to the Grand Canyon over Thanksgiving!

In other words, staying in touch with long-distance friends can literally open up your world.

# Improve Your Friendship!

Sometimes having close friendships in close spaces can create tensions of their own. If you've ever shown up to school wearing the same outfit as your best bud, you know what we mean. Oh, the humiliation! And have you and a friend ever found yourselves crushing on the same person? Yikes! But when your friend is hundreds of miles away, these problems go *poof.* Long distance friendships can provide a separation that lets both of you live your own lives without getting into too many sticky situations. You may even feel more free to pursue interests that are different from your friend's interests, because when you were together every day, you felt pressure to be into the same things.

## Get A New P.O.V.

Say you and a friend get into a huge fight. You turn to other pals for advice, but they're all too close to the situation. In this situation, a friend who lives far away can come in really handy. He or she is more likely to be able to look at the problem with fresh eyes.

## Understand That Your Friendship Will Change

All friendships change over time, whether it's with someone down the block or across the country. It may feel painful that your friend isn't around anymore for sleepovers or hanging out at the mall, and it might hurt even more when you hear about him or her making new close friends. Try not to think of your long-distance friendship as "better" or "worse" than the way it was. It's just *different*, period.

# Ways to Keep in Touch

Gone are the days of the Pony Express, when people would ride horses for days to deliver a little handwritten letter. Thank GOODNESS. Today, it's easier than ever to have virtual friendships without skipping a beat (or exhausting any ponies). You probably already know that e-mail, IM'ing, text messaging, and video chats are great ways to stay connected. Check out these other cool ideas:

**Photos:** The digital age has changed the way we document our lives with photos. Today it's snap, click, share, and post. Can't imagine getting ready for a dance without your faraway friend advising you on your outfit? Photograph yourself in each one, e-mail or text the pics to your friend, and in no time you'll know which outfit will make the biggest splash.

**Snail mail:** Does anyone send letters or postcards these days? Believe it or not, some people still prefer this "ancient" way of communicating. The great thing about snail mail is that it's so rarely used that getting a card or letter can make someone feel really excited and special. Besides... when you get something via snail mail, it's *real*. You can hold it in your hand, tape it to the inside of your locker, or file it away in a keepsake book! Keep an eye out for funny postcards that you think will give your long-distance friend a good giggle.

**Personal websites, blogs, and social networks:** If you've got a lot of friends spread out over wide spaces, you might want to think about creating a personal Web site, blog, or Facebook group. This way, you can keep friends up-to-date on the latest and greatest things going on in your life. Keep a diary, post photos, have group chats, and maybe even make some *new* friends along the way. Of course, before you post anything online you should talk to your parents to make sure you're following Internet safety guidelines and not posting too much personal information.

**Online games:** If you and your BFF love playing online games, sharing your passion from different cities is a great way to keep in touch. Whether you're kicking each other's butts in word games or building virtual worlds together, this is one part of your friendship that can still thrive.

## The Votes Are In

Have you stayed in touch with a BFF who's moved?

**No, we just couldn't make it work: 31%**
**Yes, we're just as close as ever: 44%**
Yes, but our friendship is fading: 25%

## From the Mentors

I have a friend who lives in Germany who was an exchange student at my school. We became good friends and now we correspond by sending pictures, instant messages, and e-mails. We haven't seen each other for four years and we live thousands of miles apart, but our communications are the glue that holds us together. **—LEAH**

# Get Organized!

Sometimes the best strategy for staying in touch with friends in distant places is to simply get *organized*! Try these tips for keeping the communication flowing:

**Set concrete goals**: Make a realistic goal of corresponding with your friend or friends once a month, every other month, or even just remembering a birthday... and stick to it!

**Create a friendship calendar:** Having a place where you write down important dates (like birthdays, important anniversaries, or graduations) will help you plan ahead for what's coming up. You can do this in a notebook, on a wall or desk calendar, or on your computer or phone. Electronic calendars often include reminder alarms that will give you a heads up when someone's big day is on the horizon.

**Create mailing labels on your computer**: This makes it super-easy to address letters and cards to your friends. Take it a step further and have fun adding cool fonts and art to the labels! Save your mailing lists on your computer, so if someone moves, you can update his or her address right away.

**Keep stationery and cards handy:** If you're out shopping and see the perfect card for your friend but his birthday is months away, buy it now and save it for later. See a card that you think is just really cool or funny but don't know who you'd sent it to? Snap it up anyway — you'll get the chance to send it to someone eventually. Pick out stationery that really reflects who you are, or make your own by decorating a plain sheet of paper with rubber stamps, stickers, magazine cutouts, and your own artwork.

**Keep tabs on everyone**: Try to keep all of your friends' contact info in the same place, in a cool address book, organized in your phone, or in one file on your computer. If their addresses, cell phone numbers, or e-mail addresses change, you can update your records right away.

## Remember...

Communication goes both ways. Yes, it takes two to tango, but even if your friend isn't so good at corresponding, you don't need to stop on your end. Remember that everyone goes through busy times (even you!). If someone has dropped the ball when it comes to keeping in touch, he or she will probably pick it up again when their life settles down.

# It's Your Turn!

So now that you've read through *our* advice, here's your chance to come up with some words of wisdom of your own! Pretend you're the advice columnist for your school newspaper. Copy down this question in your journal and write a response:

*I used to move a lot because my dad was in the military. Now I am moving because the place he worked at is closing. I haven't lived here very long, but I have made a really great friend.* **Lately we have hardly gotten together on the weekends or at all.** *A mutual friend tells me it's because she doesn't want to be really sad when I have to leave. What can I do?* —**AMBER, 14**

# Getting Back in Touch

Still thinking about your long-lost friend from kindergarten whose family moved away when you were six? If you're missing someone from your past, it's never too late to try and reconnect. And you never know... there's a good chance that he or she has been feeling the same way. If you're at a loss as to how to jump-start your search, try these tips:

- Check your friends of friends on your social networks, and see if any mutual friends can connect you.
- Do a white pages search or a Google search, using your friend's parents' names.
- Ask a parent or older sibling to help track down your friend's parents or older siblings through people in your community, neighborhood, or school.

## JOURNAL KICKSTART!  Keeping in Touch

Want to think deeper and express yourself about this chapter? Open up your journal, write down one or more of these sentence starters, and then see where your words and feelings take you.

- When _____ moved away, I felt...
- I keep in touch with a long distance friend by...
- The best thing about having a friend who lives far away is...
- The hardest part about it is...

# Fast Facts About My Faraway Friends

Copy this sheet or use these as examples of what details to keep on hand about friends you'd like to keep in touch with. Store them in a mobile device, your computer, or go old-school by sticking them up on a bulletin board.

Name: _____ Birthday: _____

Street Address: _____

E-mail: _____

IM address: _____

Phone numbers: _____

Especially likes: _____

Best method for us to get in touch: _____

Best times for us to talk on the phone or online: _____

Other important things to remember: _____

---

Name: _____ Birthday: _____

Street Address: _____

E-mail: _____

IM address: _____

Phone numbers: _____

Especially likes: _____

Best method for us to get in touch: _____

Best times for us to talk on the phone or online: _____

Other important things to remember: _____

# Remember...

- Don't be surprised if you find yourself feeling grief or deep sadness about being separated from a friend. That's normal and natural, so don't be ashamed to seek help if you need it.

- If a friendship meant a lot to you once, do what you can to keep it alive when the two of you are separated.

- It's easier than ever to keep in touch with faraway friends, with e-mail, instant messaging, digital photos, snail mail, and social networks. Be creative!

- Get organized! Create a friendship book or calendar that contains all of your friends' information — address, phone, e-mail address, birthdays, and so on. Then, once a month, go through the book and make a list of people to correspond with.

- Set realistic goals for how often you want to be in touch with friends. No goal is too small... even sending a birthday card once a year can be a great way to keep a friendship alive!

- Give your friend a break if he or she doesn't get back to you right away, even if you're communicating like mad.

- It's never too late to reconnect with long-lost friends. If someone's on your mind, give it a try. He or she may be just as anxious to hear from you!

# CHAPTER 8

# ENDING A FRIENDSHIP

## "It feels like we're not even friends anymore!"

## "Why is she always so mean to me?"

## "I've had enough, period. I'm done!"

We've all thought these things in the heat of conflict with a friend. (And maybe we've even cried and screamed them.) Endless fighting? Constant miscommunication? Getting treated badly? These are all things that should make you consider whether a relationship is one you still want in your life, no matter how long it's been there. That can be scary or sad to think about, but the right approach and attitude will help.

# Why Friendships End

Are you thinking about ending a friendship? It's a tough decision to make, isn't it? Hopefully, you're giving it lots of thought and taking these things into consideration:

**People Change:** Last year you were totally into online gaming. Your closest friends shared this passion, and you spent all of your time together racking up points in your favorite games. But this year, hanging out at the mall is suddenly a lot more interesting than attacking cyborgs. Your gaming friends think you're nuts. What do you do?

The truth is, we're all changing, all the time. We're changing beliefs, changing hobbies, and changing likes and dislikes. It's part of life, and especially part of life in middle school. When something about you changes, and that separates you from your friends in some way, it can cause problems. Sometimes your friends are going through changes of their own, so it won't be a big deal. You'll both move on to new friendships naturally. But every now and then, you might find yourself wanting to move on while a certain friend is standing still. He or she might try to make you feel bad for what you're going through. Don't. New differences between you and your old friend might put up a wall that's just too high to climb, and that's absolutely okay.

**Friendships Should Be Good for You:** Sure, even the most solid of friendships have some bumps in the road, but for the most part, having a friend in your life should feel *good*. So...

Is your friend good for you? Ask yourself these questions:

**Am I putting more work into this relationship than my friend?** All relationships require some give and take, but if you're the one who's always giving and your friend is always taking, things are off-balance.

**Do we have more bad times than good times together?** All relationships have their ups and downs, but what's the norm for yours?

*It's Normal for People to Come In and Out of Your Life:* Ask a parent or older relative how many times they've been through this, and they'll probably say something like, "Um, lots!" That's because regardless of your age, some friendships are just not destined to last forever but rather to serve a purpose at a certain time and place in your life. A friendship ending is not a failed friendship... it's just one that's run its natural course. (You never know: at some point in the future, because you have both changed, you and a "former friend" might circle back to each other—that's normal too!)

Remember...

Usually Great +
Sometimes Challenging =
HEALTHY FRIENDSHIP

Usually Challenging +
Sometimes Great =
UNHEALTHY FRIENDSHIP

# How to End a Friendship

**Yes, ending a friendship is hard, but it can often be the best option for everyone. It's important to handle that transition with grace, honesty, and generosity. Here's how:**

If you've decided your friendship isn't adding anything to your life, or if you just feel like the two of you don't have anything in common anymore, it's time to close the door. This might sound scary, but it doesn't have to be. Follow these two steps as you make your plan:

## Think

Think about the reasons behind your decision to call it quits, and make sure it's based on more than just raw emotions or the heat of the moment. *I-Messages* can help you get it straight in your head:

**1. I feel...** _____

**2. When you...** _____

3. Because... _____.

You can also check in with parents or older siblings, and share your decision with them. At a time like this, you need the support of people who have *your* best interests at heart. Maybe they can even offer you advice or insight you might not have thought of on your own.

## Talk

Talk with your friend and tell him or her what's going on. As hard as it might be, stay calm and cool and avoid blaming the other person. Remember… this decision is about *you*. Here are some ways you could start your conversation:

- "I don't think we should spend as much time together right now because _____."
- "I've given it a lot of thought, and I'd like to take a break from our friendship."

Your friend might be shocked and press you for more information or even try to change your mind. You can explain your reasons, but again, try not to place blame or say hurtful things. You've already made the tough call. There's no point in making your friend feel any worse.

If you've thought about the situation and approached it in a careful, well-considered way, be at peace with your decision. Your friend, or ex-friend, might need more time to adjust, and that's okay. Be sensitive to how he or she might react, but stand firm. At the end of the day, you're only responsible for one person's emotions, and those are *yours*. Your friend will need to go through his or her own process of feelings and reactions.

Don't be surprised if one of your friend's reactions is anger and the need for "revenge." Your friend might lash out by spreading rumors about you or trying to get other people to side with him or her. If that happens, try not to be intimidated and stick by your decision. Take another read through the When Friends Fight and Gossip and Rumors chapters of this book!

## Remember...

If you're sticking with a friend who doesn't make you feel good, the friendship will never be the kind that truly satisfies you. Rather than going down that path, concentrate on finding friendships that are more fulfilling. It might take a while, but in the long run, you'll be much better off.

## What comes next

When the dust settles, it's natural to feel regret ("OMG, what did I just do?"), sadness, and even grief. After all, ending a friendship is a loss. Even when you know it's for the best, the experience can be tough and painful.

Take a pause to remember — or even better, record in your journal — the best memories of this friendship. Arrange to spend more time with other friends and embrace the possibility of getting closer to them. Seek out fresh friendships (see the How To Make Friends chapter) if you feel that's what you need.

You may also want to figure out how you're going to react to seeing and being around your former friend from now on. Because you *know* that's going to happen. If you can agree on something with the other person—such as, saying "hi" in school—that's ideal. In the end, however, it's up to you to determine your own behavior. Think about what feels most comfortable, but also keep in mind that ignoring or avoiding someone can be a lot harder (and feel much more awful) than it sounds. See if you can find a middle ground that works for you... and hopefully the other person, too.

Finally, to echo what we said earlier: don't let yourself think of your ended friendship as a "mistake," "disaster," or "failure." Instead, try framing it as a relationship that ran its course, at least for the time being... and feel proud that you made choices that kept you true to yourself.

# It's Your Turn!

So now that you've read through *our* advice, here's your chance to come up with some words of wisdom of your own! Pretend you're the advice columnist for your school newspaper. Copy down this question in your journal and write a response:

*My friend David and I have been best friends for a long time, and our moms are good friends, too. This past year, we have definitely grown apart and don't get along so well, mostly because he joined the soccer team and is really into that, and I'm not. I have also started hanging out with some new people who I really like. Recently I found out he was telling some of his teammates secrets about me. Is it time for us to end our friendship? It could be a weird situation because of our moms.* —JAKE, 12

## JOURNAL KICKSTART! Ending a Friendship

Want to think deeper and express yourself about this chapter? Open up your journal, write down one or more of these sentence starters, and then see where your words and feelings take you.

- It's time to end my friendship with _____ because...
- My friendship with _____ makes me unhappy because...
- The most important things to me in a friend are...
- I know that after ending this friendship I will be fine because...
- After I end my friendship, I'll feel... _____ .

## Quotes From Kids Like You

*"When me and my ex-best friend would fight, we would get really mad at each other and not talk. We usually made up, but one day she pushed me over the edge, and I told her that we shouldn't be friends anymore."*

**—ALLIE, 12**

*"My two closest friends live in the same neighborhood and I live in a different neighborhood. **When they are together they leave me out, so now we're not really friends!***

**—LINDSEY, 12**

*"Me and my friend always fight. But when a friend keeps pushing it to the point where you can't handle it, maybe it's time to move on."*

**—STEVEN, 13**

## From the Mentors

Basically, it's time to end a friendship when you realize that somehow, you're headed in two completely different directions and there's no way for it to be solved. Before ending the friendship, try to understand what happened between you. It can make it easier to move forward if you understand what went on. Try to meet new friends, instead of staying upset about the loss of your old friend. **—MEGAN**

It's time to call a friendship quits when you feel emotionally or physically abused. For instance, if you can't sleep for a long period of time, or you're constantly depressed over it. Or if he or she calls you names and makes fun of you, or if you hurt more then you smile, or if you can't remember a single good time. Talk to your friend. If they make no effort at all to make things better — END IT RIGHT NOW. A bad friend isn't a friend at all. **—JESSICA**

## Remember...

Don't feel guilty about wanting to explore new things. That's part of figuring out who you are! If your friends don't like the new you, give it time. You'll eventually meet people who share your new passions.

# Has Your Friendship Run Its Course?

**Think about which statements apply to you and your friend, then compare the two lists.**

## The Good Stuff

- I know I can trust my friend with a secret.
- My friend and I share a lot of likes and dislikes.
- My friend gives great advice when I need it, and is good at making me feel better when I'm down.
- I feel like my friend would stick up for me if other people were putting me down.
- When something good happens to me, my friend is almost as happy as I am.

## The Bad Stuff

- My friend and I have some misunderstandings that lead to fights.
- Sometimes my friend pressures me or tells me what to do.
- Sometimes my friend makes fun of me or puts me down in front of other people.
- Sometimes my friend gossips or spreads rumors about me.
- Sometimes my friend seems to "control" me by knowing just what to do or say.
- My friend gets jealous or competitive with me really easily, and it's usually over stupid things.

## From the Mentors

I believe you should try everything possible to fix a friendship before calling it quits, and if you do pull through, then you grow even closer to that friend. But if you really have to take a break or end the friendship for now, it may not be for good. Sometimes TIME is what heals. **—JARON**

- I feel like I can tell my friend anything without him or her judging me.
- When I'm with my friend, I totally feel like myself.
- I can count on my friend to be honest with me at all times.
- My friend and I laugh a lot and share the same sense of humor.
- My friend and I have a lot of history and great memories.
- I can't imagine not having my friend in my life. If our friendship ended, I'm not sure I would ever get over it.

- Occasionally, my friend seems happy when something bad happens to me.
- My friend gets insulted when I don't want to spend time together, and can be a bit clingy.
- I feel like I can't completely be myself around my friend, or that there are things about me that I don't want him or her to find out.
- I'm just not interested in the same things my friend is anymore, and we don't have much to talk about.
- If our friendship ended, I would be sad, but I think I would get over it.

## Remember...

- People change and so do friendships... it's a normal part of life.

- Don't feel guilty for expanding your interests and friendships into new areas.

- If you have more bad times than good with your friend, it might be time to end the friendship.

- Bad friends are NOT better than no friends at all.

# CONCLUSION

## Whew.

So, yeah. We meant it when we said that friendships are never simple. They take *work*! But now you have the right information and tools for the job. We hope that during the daily ins and outs and ups and downs with your friends, you're able to remember that:

- **Friends are people who make you feel good about yourself, like you for who you are, and are there for you during the bad times as well as the good.**

- **The more friends you have of different types — from close friends to casual acquaintances to protégés — the more satisfied you'll be.** Sometimes you have to overcome shyness and other obstacles to build this circle of friends, but there are lots of ways to do it. Even far away friends can add something unique to your life.

- Fighting is normal... but if you deal with it in a positive, proactive way, your friendships will grow stronger as a result. Understanding how hurtful gossip and rumors can be, and knowing how to break their chains, will help you keep peace among your friends. Make **"Think, Talk, Apologize, Move On"** and **"I-Messages"** part of your toolbox.

- Healthy friendships are **"Usually Great, Sometimes Challenging"**; unhealthy friendships are the other way around. If you have a friend who's always getting mad at you, pressures you, disrespects you, controls you, clings too close, or is always jealous of you... well, it might be time to take a long hard look at whether that relationship is right for you. Although it can be painful, sometimes you have to accept that a friendship is over and you need to move on.

Yup, friendship takes work, but it's totally worth it... if the results are friendships that are strong, healthy, long-lasting, and ones that make everything else in your life better.

# We wish these friendships to all of you!

Hey, are you wondering where the kid and "Mentor" comments in this book came from? And who voted in all those polls, anyway? These contributions came from visitors to *It's My Life*, the PBS Kids website about "real life" topics such as family, school, emotions, and... you guessed it: friends.

**JENNIFER CASTLE** is the creator and producer of "It's My Life," the award-winning PBS Kids website for tweens. She's also the author of two novels for young adults, *You Look Different in Real Life* and *The Beginning of After*, both published by HarperCollins. She lives in New York's Hudson Valley with her husband, two daughters, two cats... and a pretty awesome family of friends.

**DEBORAH REBER** is an accomplished author for tweens and teens. A former children's television executive, Deborah uses her writing, speaking, and volunteering work to inspire girls everywhere to live their best life. Deborah is the author of *Doable: The Girl's Guide to Accomplishing Just About Anything, Chill: Stress Reducing Techniques for a More Balanced, Peaceful You,* and *In Their Shoes, Extraordinary Women Describe Their Amazing Careers.* She lives in Amsterdam, The Netherlands, with her husband, son, and cat.

**KAELA GRAHAM** is an illustrator and designer living in Seattle, where she divides her time between working on creative projects and going on outdoor adventures with her little dog.